The Art of Column Writing

The Art of Column Writing

Insider Secrets

from
Art Buchwald,
Dave Barry,
Arianna Huffington,
Pete Hamill
and other great
columnists

Suzette Martinez Standring

Marion Street Press
Portland, Oregon

*To The Man Upstairs who brought me to all this for a reason,
and to my husband David and daughter Star who remind me
what it is.*

ISBN 1-933338-261
ISBN 13: 978-1-933338-262
Printed in U.S.A.
Printing 11 10 9 8 7 6 5 4 3 2

Marion Street Press
4326 S.E. Woodstock Blvd. # 406
Portland, Ore. 97206-6270
(503) 888-4624
www.marionstreetpress.com

Contents

7 Prologue

9 Introduction: The Quest for a Column

Section 1: The How-To of Column Writing

13 Point of View

18 Voice

28 Beginnings

33 Telling the Story

43 Putting Endings First

48 Column Length

51 Writing Tips From Two Columnists

55 The Big, Bad, Blank Screen

61 On Copyright

65 Working With Editors

71 Self-Editing: Your Machete or Mine?

75 Elements of a Pulitzer Prize-Winning Column

81 The Making of a Columnist

Section 2: Specialty Columns

88   The Humor Columnist

99   The Lifestyle Columnist

110   The Metro Columnist

115   The Opinion Columist

121   The Religion Columnist

133   Niche Columns

Section 3: A Columnist's Inner World

138   Who Are These People?

144   Ethics

155   Can a Columnist Have Friends?

Section 4: What Lies Beyond the Column

162   Oh, the Places You'll Go With a Column

165   Syndication

173   Blogging

179   Radio: On the Air With Columnists

185   Journalism and Standup Comedy:
There is a Difference

191   Onward

Prologue

Every morning millions of readers turn the page to their favorite newspaper columnist. Maybe turning your stories or opinions into a column has crossed your mind.

This is why I know this book will be helpful.

Within a short time from when I first began my freelance column in 2000, my work went from an occasional run to frequent newspaper publication. In 2003 I was voted Best Columnist by the readership of *The Milton Times* (Mass.). In 2005, the year I first approached *The Boston Globe*, they ran all three columns I submitted. In 2006, *The Patriot Ledger* (Mass.) made me one of their regular Faith and Values columnists on its religion page. That same year, I wrote a column about spending two days in hospice with Art Buchwald that was carried widely on national news sites and was featured on Boston's NPR affiliate.

What made the difference? Learning from colleagues I met through the National Society of Newspaper Columnists, America's oldest and largest organization devoted solely to newspaper columnists. I joined the NSNC in 1999 and became its president for the 2004-2006 term.

In comparison, my colleagues can roll out mightily more impressive resumes. But considering my background — no college degree and no formal training in writing — my progress is stunning and I credit colleagues who were generous with their advice.

From working columnists I learned about writing with all five senses, how to discern one's true voice, how to work with editors, and how to keep things fresh. In trying to understand their success, I poked and prodded at their greatness. They, in turn, nudged me toward being great, too. I am a work in progress, but my milestones were unthinkable back when I first tiptoed into a hotel ballroom swarming with professional columnists.

They gave me much more than a practical primer on how to write, and that was how to *be*.

Truthful. Real. Using one's sensibilities to help others understand the world around them, or better yet, how to change that little part of the world each of us can reach.

It occurred to me that if their advice propelled my career forward, then why not mine that rich vein for others? Maybe you're just starting out and need advice. If you're a seasoned columnist, then be refreshed.

Here working columnists share their secrets to column writing success. Be inspired by the passion of some of the finest in the industry for this unique and beloved genre.

Suzette Martinez Standring
Past President
National Society of Newspaper Columnists
July 11, 2007

Therefore search and see if there is not some place where you may invest your humanity.

The Quest for a Column

Columns are concentrated storytelling, and you dream of writing a great one. Your work moves people to action. Thanks to you, stubborn contrarians change long-held beliefs. Readers laugh or cry, but certainly they ask their friends, "Did you read her column this morning?"

This is your dream.

Invariably, the quest begins with the question, "How do I become a columnist?"

Here's the deal: many arrived at their careers through strange and inexplicable circumstances, which makes sense because columnists are strange and inexplicable people. Few began with "columnist" as their ultimate writing goal. Many were writers on their way to other things — news reporters, music critics, authors, or feature writers. One columnist got his start as a regular generator of "letters to the editor." The Kingdom of Columnists is fraught with zigs and zags.

Before newspaper writing, I was an association director in California, my home state. My writing experience came mainly from promoting legal seminars and penning persuasive letters to big shot attorneys. Long comical letters to friends rounded out my writing resume.

When my husband's pharmaceutical career relocated us to New Jersey in 1998, I saw an ad for an adult education class in journalism.

"Hey, writing as a career," I thought, "No more lawyers. Yeah."

Jay Langley, the then owner/editor of the *Hunterdon County Democrat*, taught the basics of news writing with six weeks of practice articles. Langley was impressed with my "homework" and suggested I work for him.

It all happened so fast. I went from wowing him with a mushroom hunting feature to becoming the county news reporter.

"Wait," I said, "I'm not familiar with New Jersey yet. County politics? No way. County fairs, maybe."

Langley said, "You'll get it through osmosis."

He waved me off, even as my plaintive question echoed down the hallway, "What's a board of freeholders?" (the county board of elected officials, as I soon learned).

So I tackled open space preservation and local elections. I became the point person on the deer overpopulation problem. I, who had no previous experience with wild animals, soon became an expert of deer biology, infrared aerial surveys, crop loss, and Lyme disease.

So I penned a humor column as personal therapy. My perspective was the citified woman now living in an agricultural New Jersey suburb. I wrote about things like seeing deer for the first time. There I was, jumping up and down, shiny-eyed with excitement as if they were gorillas. In contrast, my neighbors couldn't even bother to look up from their coffee cups, long jaded as they were from hordes of deer munching on their lawns.

Cooking up these columns was a way to kill time before the county meetings started. On impulse, I handed one to the editor, and asked, "What do you think?"

Langley said, "Not bad, I'll run it."

It became a popular feature.

Later, I relocated to Boston and brought with me my new passion for column writing. This time, I decided to give freelance writing a try.

I joined the National Society of Newspaper Columnists, looking to them to shine a light on the straight road to a career in column writing.

Guess what? It doesn't exist.

According to colleagues, this is how they got their jobs: a freak accident, hard work, being-at-the-right-place-at-the-right-time-with-the-right-subject, good contacts, sheer serendipity, having a column added to news reporting duties, answering an ad, building a saleable body of work, networking, wearing down an editor, developing a readership separate from a newspaper, writing a book, becoming an expert, or just plain dumb luck.

Many stood by their plan (or lack of one) and swore success, but here's the real lowdown: every triumph was based on stellar writing.

Which leads to another question commonly asked during one's quest for a column — "Where can I get my work published?"

Certainly, as a novice, that was my own Holy Grail question.

Much to my chagrin, I discovered it is a cart-before-the-horse query.

It is better to ask, "How can I make my work worthy of being published?"

Let's take a moment to deconstruct a newspaper column.

It compels or captivates with a tale, a message, or a persuasive argument. Jam-pack those thoughts into, say, 600 select words. Create an engaging start, an informative middle, and ideally, a surprise ending, all written in a voice so signature any reader could identify the columnist even without a byline.

"What we do is more like a short story," said legendary metro columnist Pete Hamill during a 2005 NSNC meeting in Texas.

Time, talent, and practice are required to do condensed writing well.

The aspiring columnist often seeks a tried-and-true writing formula. Is there an ideal format or length? Is it better to cover up-to-the-minute issues or write about subjects with shelf life?

One size cannot possibly fit all, considering that columns can range from politics to parenthood and everything in between. Insights into specialty subjects are helpful, but the one bond among columnists (and true hope for publication) is a passion for excellent writing.

Let's not begin with, "What newspapers might run my column?"

Instead, let's find ways to answer the question, "How can I make my columns outstanding?"

What follows is the best advice from award-winning columnists.

Section 1: The How-To of Column Writing

A definite purpose, like blinders on a horse, inevitably narrows its possessor's point of view.

Robert Frost

Point of View

Wanted: a strong, personal point of view, emphasis on "personal." No other form of journalism but column writing allows the writer's individuality to shape both a message and a self-portrait.

Viewpoint is different from "voice." Voice is the writing style of the columnist. Point of view is the writer's perspective, her fixed identity in print. For example, readers expected columnist Molly Ivins' point of view to be politically liberal, while her writing voice conveys a "don't-this-beat-all" sense of humor.

Clear examples of point-of-view writing can be found in commentary where one's politics color personal opinion. Advice columnists offer their special slant on handling life's problems. Humorists personalize their view of a world gone awry.

Personal bias is acceptable in column writing. In fact, objectivity is not required, according to a majority of columnists polled in a survey by the National Society of Newspaper Columnists. A columnist is not expected to give equal weight to both sides of an issue.

However, in offering written bias, a columnist is obligated to support it with facts. Project passion, but keep it fair with research and accuracy because readers look to a columnist's viewpoint for help in interpreting events or forming opinions.

"It requires you to be almost like a lawyer. Through your arguments, you will need to convince the jury (your readers) that your client (your viewpoint) is right. Shaping a powerful argument takes practice and requires both breadth and depth of knowledge as well as the ability to critically analyze a particular issue," wrote Oon Yeoh, a writing consultant and columnist for *Today*, a Singapore daily, and *The Edge*, a Malaysian business weekly.

Walter Brasch is a journalism and mass communications professor and author of a biweekly syndicated newspaper column. A recipient of numerous journalism awards, Brasch offers two point-of-view tips:

■ Fight homogeneous style: Don't imitate popular columnists. Offer readers something different. "Too often columnists read each other and they start to write like each other," he says.

■ Don't modify your message: Your audience is the reader. Don't adjust your message to please editors or just to get published. Editors fail their readers when they expect writers to mirror the styles of big newspaper columnists.

"The problem is convincing editors they need to have a vast number of views from all parts of the country from all kinds of writers," says Brasch.

An original viewpoint is irresistible. Columnist Robin Givhan of *The Washington Post* won the 2006 Pulitzer Prize for Criticism. This was a first-ever for a fashion columnist.

Givhan has covered an international global fashion industry, presidential inaugurals, and the Academy Awards as an editor and columnist for *The Washington Post* since 1995. Previously, she worked for *Vogue*, *The Detroit Free Press* and *The San Francisco Chronicle*.

Her fashion column is popular for its unique point of view: What subliminal messages do politicians and celebrities seek to send by wearing certain clothes? She reveals their fashion choices as symbolism, façade, crusade, faux pas, or disrespect.

"Gown watch" during the second Clinton inaugural was her light-bulb moment, when Washington politics and fashion came together to create her column's point of view.

Givhan says, "I asked myself, why do we care so much about what this gown looks like? I wrote a piece about it and realized the first lady's role and her clothes are so symbolic.

"Being first lady is not defined as a job with something specific you have to do, other than essentially represent the American people. As a symbol, as a package, you want her to reflect the best of what we think of ourselves as being. That helped me understand better why the inaugural gown was something significant.

"There are a lot of little moments like when candidates visit factories and take off their coats, roll up their sleeves and talk to blue collar guys. It's the visual language of, 'Hey, I'm a regular guy.'

"I make a unique connection between attire and its national or cultural message. I tell people about the power of that type of symbolism."

Every columnist, novice or seasoned, holds a unique point of view because our outlook is the sum of our personal experiences. No one else in the world has led your life, so all your observations are uniquely enriched.

Brasch adds, "Everything that has gone into a writer's life from birth to the present helps to develop a point of view. Whenever somebody asks me how long it took me to write a book or column, I say all my life."

Here is an example of a column written from a unique point of view.

An Image a Little Too Carefully Coordinated

By Robin Givhan, The Washington Post
Friday, July 22, 2005

It has been a long time since so much syrupy nostalgia has been in evidence at the White House. But Tuesday night, when President Bush announced his choice for the next associate justice of the Supreme Court, it was hard not to marvel at the 1950s-style *tableau vivant* that was John Roberts and his family.

There they were — John, Jane, Josie and Jack — standing with the president and before the entire country. The nominee was in a sober suit with the expected white shirt and red tie. His wife and children stood before the cameras, groomed and glossy in pastel hues — like a trio of Easter eggs, a handful of Jelly Bellies, three little Necco wafers. There was tow-headed Jack — having freed himself from the controlling grip of his mother — enjoying a moment in the spotlight dressed in a seersucker suit with short pants and saddle shoes. His sister, Josie, was half-hidden behind her mother's skirt. Her blond pageboy glistened. And she was wearing a yellow dress with a crisp white collar, lace-trimmed anklets and black patent-leather Mary Janes.

(Who among us did a double take? Two cute blond children with a boyish-looking father getting ready to take the lectern — Jack Edwards? Emma Claire? Is that you? Are *all* little boys now named Jack?)

The wife wore a strawberry-pink tweed suit with taupe pumps and pearls, which alone would not have been particularly remarkable, but alongside the nostalgic costuming of the children, the overall effect was of self-consciously crafted perfection. The children, of course, are innocents. They are dressed by their parents. And through their clothes choices, the parents have created the kind of honeyed faultlessness that jams mailboxes every December when personalized Christmas cards arrive bringing greetings "to you and yours" from the Blake family or the Joneses. Everyone looks freshly scrubbed and adorable, just like they have stepped from a Currier & Ives landscape.

In a time when most children are dressed in Gap Kids and retailers of similar price-point and modernity, the parents put young master Jack in an ensemble that calls to mind John F. "John-John" Kennedy Jr.

Separate the child from the clothes, which do not acknowledge trends, popular culture or the passing of time. They are not classic; they are old-fashioned. These clothes are Old World, old money and a cut above the light-up-shoe-buying hoi polloi.

The clothes also reflect a bit of the aesthetic havoc that often occurs when people visit the White House. (What should I wear? How do I look? Take my picture!) The usual advice is to *dress appropriately.* In this case, an addendum would have been helpful: Please select all attire from the commonly accepted styles of this century. (And someone should have given notice to the flip-flop-wearing women of Northwestern University's lacrosse team, who visited the White House on July 12 for a meet-and-greet with the president: proper footwear required. Flip-flops, modeled after shoes meant to be worn into a public shower or on the beach, have no business anywhere in the vicinity of the president and his place of residence.)

Dressing appropriately is a somewhat selfless act. It's not about catering to personal comfort. One can't give in fully to private aesthetic preferences. Instead, one asks what would make other people feel respected? What would mark the occasion as noteworthy? What signifies that the moment is bigger than the individual?

But the Roberts family went too far. In announcing John Roberts as his Supreme Court nominee, the president inextricably linked the individual — and his family — to the sweep of tradition. In their attire, there was nothing too informal; there was nothing immodest. There was only the feeling that, in the desire to be appropriate and respectful of history, the children had been costumed in it.

Reprinted with permission of The Washington Post

Style is knowing who you are, what you want to say and not giving a damn.

Gore Vidal

Voice

The Pied Piper in column writing seduces readers with a memorable voice. Voice is the writer's personality on the printed page, the style in which a point of view is conveyed. Voice allows the reader to see the world through the writer's lens, creating a sense of intimacy. A columnist has successfully created a voice when strangers in a supermarket say, "I feel like I know you."

At the start of my writing career I knew nothing about a writing voice. Very green to newspaper work in 1998, I was busy grasping the who-what-when-where-how-and-why of news reporting. Assigned to cover county news was like being plunked into a pilot's seat and told, "Land this thing!"

A newsroom is a busy place, and typically no one is available for constant mentoring. Occasionally, drops of wisdom spatter down like rain, and if you keep an ear cocked, you might catch some. The first time I heard about "voice" was when a humor column was added to my duties.

The editor said, "Keep your column down to 500 words."

"How do I do that?"

"Write tight and don't be redundant. You have a good voice."

Hmm. I stood in the hallway, completely stumped. I thought he meant my "vocal" voice, which made no sense because he didn't hear mine very often.

Eventually, when I caught on to the concept of a writing voice, my concerns grew. Is my voice good enough? Can I improve its style? If I hear various voices in my head, does it mean

I own different writing voices? (Uh oh, is it safe to reveal that?)

This seemingly lone columnist in the wilderness happily discovered that many others before me had collected answers in their own desert wanderings.

Is That Voice Yours or Mine?

"Voice is what makes a column good and personal," says editor L. Kim Tan of *The Boston Globe.*

Every writer is concerned with authenticity, so is there a formula for creating a memorable voice? No, not any more than someone can hand you a personality. It is not an act of creation but an exercise in development. Writing is a craft. Think of your voice as a rough-cut gem with a potential for brilliant facets.

As a novice, I heard award-winning writers' voices described as "unique" or "authentic," even "courageous." This made me very nervous. Like a new mother concerned with a maternity ward mix-up, I questioned whether the voice I had was truly my own. Was I a wannabe version of someone else? Is it kosher to imitate an admired writer?

Smelling salts arrived in the form of advice from veteran columnists. Emulation is not a form of personality plagiarism. It is common to follow the lead of much-loved authors, especially at the beginning of a writing career. Consider them case studies in developing your own voice — even if they write about interests wildly different from your own.

For example, Thomas Friedman's foreign policy columns and my wacky work have little connection, but I've learned much from his ability to simplify complexities in a manner respectful to the reader.

Mary McCarty pens a thrice-weekly column for the *Dayton Daily News* and is syndicated through Cox News Service. Her awards include the H.L. Mencken Award, Writer of the Year for Cox Newspapers, and Best Columnist in Ohio by the Ohio Chapter of the Society of Professional Journalists.

"How I learned to write is being a voracious reader all my life. I like to read writers who have achieved a level I will never achieve, such as Shakespeare, Margaret Atwood, or Toni Morrison. That kind of writing is ennobling and it's humbling. Don't worry about being the world's best writer; that's already been taken," said McCarty at a 2006 Erma Bombeck Writers' Workshop in Dayton, Ohio.

The memorable work of others can serve as mini-tutorials for developing personal style, according to Oon Yeoh, a writing consultant and current affairs columnist for *Today,* a Singapore daily.

"Follow the work of several established columnists and analyze their writings to discover how they project their arguments and how they make effective use of anecdotes, quotes, and statistics. From there, you can learn the tricks of the trade and eventually develop your own distinctive voice and style," he says.

No One Style Reigns Supreme

In the stop-and-compare process, it's easy to be intimidated by extraordinary work. Pause. Breathe deeply. Settle into your own writing skin and view it simply as a spur toward personal originality.

Each voice will reveal its own natural flair over time. Some write sentences full of bends, dips and eddies. Others are to the point. Whether sweeping or staccato, the style of a writer should rebel against formula.

"Language is like music. Don't buy into the 'keep it simple, stupid,'" said McCarty.

Meek Person, Passionate Voice

Writing personas and real-life personalities do not always match. Often, those who boldly bare themselves on a page are quite shy in person. The writer of poetic prose is not always a great conversationalist. Not uncommon is the social justice crusader who hates socializing.

For the record, a strong personality does not equal a strong writing voice. Happily, the writing realm decrees that even the meekest among us can possess great power with language and imagery.

Strut your stuff with subjects you care about. Politics? Parenthood? Health? Music? The vroom-vroom of voice revs up on a good ride. Without passion, your column's byline may be fleeting.

In my early days of freelancing, I sorely wanted a spot as a humor columnist. Instead, *The Patriot Ledger* tagged me to write *In The Shops*, a column that featured three gift items weekly. A regular byline thrilled me and I reasoned, "Finally, somebody is paying me to shop."

But my "voice" wasn't meant for that type of column. How long could I cleverly craft descriptions of glass trays and mosaic tables? The tedium wore me down like a pack mule in the Mojave, and months later I begged off.

Important lesson: write about what excites you or it won't

last.

Likewise, do not create a column solely based on a perceived readership demand. While it is true there is a market for specialty columns, such as technology and science, a personal interest is vital. Otherwise, readers will see through the façade, and nothing sinks a column faster than a lackluster voice.

Owner to Voice: Come In, Come In.

Do you remember *The Velveteen Rabbit*, a children's story about the toy longing to come alive? Perhaps a frayed little critter within each of us wonders when the voice within us becomes "real." How do various columnists discern their real voice from an inner poseur?

For me, authenticity is triggered by a physical sensation. While drafting a humor column, my inner voice leans forward, mightily amused, and throws out a chunk of irony. Plunk! It ripples into ever-widening comedic circles and I write as I laugh, listening to a quick-talking storyteller voice in my head. There is a physical sensation in my gut.

Award-winning columnist Tracey O'Shaughnessy pens lifestyle columns for the *Republican American* in Connecticut.

"There is, I think, a voice in all of us that reacts to life as a continuous monologue. That's the voice we hear inside our heads when we are writing. It's not necessarily the voice you use while speaking; in fact, it is usually quite unlike it, but it is the voice we hear while thinking, a voice that is as singular as we are," says O'Shaughnessy.

Conversely, for Karen Rinehart, a self-syndicated humorist, her inner and out-loud voices are the same. Her column, *Bus Stop Mommies*, appears in the *Independent Tribune* (NC) and other papers.

"I've been told I write like I talk, which is a compliment since I can't spell-check, backspace, or delete the erroneous junk that easily slips out of my mouth. The conversational style is an easy or comfortable read for many folks," she says.

Ellen Goodman of *The Boston Globe* believes the trick to releasing her inner voice is by speaking aloud.

"I definitely have the same writing and speaking voice. In fact I move my lips while I write. Which may sound like fourth grade but it's true. I like to hear the words I'm writing. A lot of people talk about finding a voice as if it were in a pumpkin patch, or in someone else's work. I think of it as letting the voice that is yours out," Goodman says.

A quiet space allows voice to emerge, according to Ron Jackson, a columnist with the *Kankakee Daily Journal* (IL).

"I have a technique. I close my eyes before I write. That gives me the illusion no one is around to hear what I'm thinking. Then I just say what's on my mind. I write like I talk. That helps when people meet you in public. They know it's you when you use the same words and style as you do in print," says Jackson.

Sometimes voice can be an idealized version of self, according to Rick Epstein, a long-time family columnist, author, and editor for the *Hunterdon County* (NJ) *Democrat.*

"My voice would be a kind of 'Rick perfected,' and that idea of perfection is real and genuinely mine because not everybody prizes the same qualities or has the same role models. My voice draws from the things I liked about Fess Parker as Davy Crockett, Jimmy Stewart, my professorial father, or Sean Connery as James Bond," says Epstein.

Workout and Write

Voice gets its definition from a regular workout, so write, write, and write some more. Isn't that a disappointing tip? Don't you wish there were an easier way? Sadly, the "voice quest" does not lead to perfection via a magic zap to the brain. No, it occurs on the other end. Velcro your butt to the chair.

Keep to a schedule and spend the best creative zone of your day at the computer screen. A regular habit strengthens your voice and daily results will grow a sellable body of work.

Waiting for the mood to strike is not practiced among professionals. Like potty training, success won't come with a "whatever happens, happens" approach. Schedule time to write. Show up and get tapping. Answer to somebody else and share your work.

"When you do anything often enough — music, painting, basketball — you develop your own style," says syndicated columnist David V. Chartrand.

Your Writing Voice Wants to Sing

If your shoulders sag at the thought of tick-tock-tick-tock tethered to a screen, then buck up. Columnists have playful ways to coax their voices onto the page, too.

For instance, have you ever thought of pegging your writing voice to a song? The idea came from Dr. Roy Peter Clark, the vice president and senior scholar at The Poynter Institute. He's a piano playin' man.

"If your column had an entrance song, what would it be?" Clark asked NSNC columnists in 2004 at New Orleans.

Clark played various piano rhythms to demonstrate how writing, like music, can set a mood. He was not suggesting columnists draft columns to music, but rather how the use of words and sentence structure can create a personal writing rhythm.

Do you employ short sentences or a flowing stream of prose?

How does melody play in your writing voice?

Chatty? Nostalgic? Combative?

Clark played a mixture of melodies to conjure up different moods.

What feeling does your writing convey?

What emotion is evoked from a reader?

If your column could be matched to a tune, what song embodies your style?

Columnists in the audience yelled out, *"Positively Fourth Street!"* or *"For Once in My Life,"* or *"Werewolf of London!"* (*"The Bitch is Back!" was refreshingly candid.*)

Every time my column runs, it feels like *At Last* by Etta James, but if I want to be buck naked honest, I fear my worst writing days produce *Yummy, Yummy, Yummy, I've Got Love in My Tummy.*

Read Your Work Out Loud

To fine-tune voice, use yours. Like music, the flow of words is best judged by the sense of hearing. Read your work out loud. Badly chosen words, repetition, and awkward phrases are quickly obvious to the ear. Likewise, the lilt and melody of language come alive when spoken.

Art Buchwald said, "I don't read it out loud, I'm singing it. I want rhythm in my column and words are rhythm."

Pete Hamill is an award-winning columnist, journalist, and author. At a 2005 NSNC meeting in Texas, he shared a jazz tip he applies to his own writing.

As a young journalist, he read an interview with drummer Gene Krupa, in which he was asked how he kept time for the band. The musician shared his secret phrase:

"Lyonnaise potatoes and some pork chops."

Krupa would repeat this to himself while performing.

Hamill made a connection to writing. A story needs cadence, timing, and a lively beat to come alive.

"Even if it's just 'one dead, two hurt in car crash,' " says Hamill.

On the following pages, two columnists write about the same topic in different voices.

An Open Letter on Thanksgiving

By George Waters

The following is an open letter to the president of the United States.

Dear Mr. President,

My name is Tom, and I am a turkey.

You may be wondering how I learned to type. Believe me, when 97 percent of Americans say they plan to eat you Thursday, it's a powerful motivator.

I am writing because I would like to apply for the annual turkey anemsty, amnyty, sorry, amnesty (it's hard to type without opposable thumbs) which you so graciously offer one turkey each year at the White House. "Pardoning the turkey," I believe you call it.

Ha ha, that is funny, sir. It sure is funny to "pardon" a bird who has done nothing wrong, but is facing death. Ha ha, good one, Mr. President.

Hold on, my wattle got in my eyes.

O.K., seriously, Mr. P, this week, millions of my friends will be sacrificed to the "celebration" you call "Thanksgiving." Forgive my audacity, sir, but we turkeys have another name for it. We call it "Black Thursday." You have recently affirmed your stance against torture, Mr. P, but you apparently have no qualms about poultry genocide. Do I sense a paradox?

Sure, people think turkeys are stupid. People think, 'Oooh, they're so fat and so stupid, let's eat them.'

Hypocrites.

You don't see them eating members of Congress, do you?

And people are incredibly closed-minded about Thanksgiving menu alternatives. Walk into a bar and mention turkey substitutes like "Tofurkey" (delicious turkey-flavored tofu) or "UnTurkey" (turkey-shaped wheat gluten, yum!) and all you get is laughter. Believe me, I've tried.

Have you ever been called "Butterball," Mr. President? It stings.

Listen, give me this year's pardon, and you will be doing some hungry family a favor. Trust me, I am tough and stringy.

I smoked for many years.

I can suck down a bag of pork rinds in two minutes flat, and I drink more Wild Turkey in a week than most wild turkeys knock back in a year.

My liver is shot.

You don't want to see my giblets, believe me.

I am no free-range, grain-fed turkey. I have always had a weakness for cheeseburgers.

If ever there was a guy who did not belong on a platter next to yams, it is me. It is I. (Sorry, I learned English from a chicken.)

I am appealing to your patriotism, Mr. President. Benjamin Franklin wanted the turkey to be America's national bird, and it's not too late to make that happen. You could push it through! No way the Democrats would filibuster that. PETA would be all over them faster than a rescued greyhound on a pork chop.

Or how about this—you pardon me, and I work with you on undermining the Democratic Party. Picture this: on election eve, we turkeys give them all salmonella. It could work! We could call it Plan T. Anyway, think about it. Talk to Karl.

Mr. President, on Thursday, Americans will eat 675 million pounds of trkuey, er, turkey (sorry, that number makes me a little woozy). I am requesting your help in making that total about 20 pounds less.

Please, sir! If I could reach my wishbone, I'd be yanking that sucker silly right now. Do this for me, and I will obediently live out my days letting schoolchildren pet me on that farm in Virginia where the pardoned birds go.

My tail is in your hands, sir. If you decide not to pardon me, well, just stick one of those little plastic pop-up thermometers in me, I'm done.

Sincerely,

Tom
A turkey of, by, but hopefully not for, the people

Reprinted by permission

Meanwhile: Chacun à son goût on Thanksgiving

By Art Buchwald

The Turkey Growers Association has approved this message.

One of our most important holidays is Thanksgiving Day, known in France as le Jour de Merci Donnant.

Le Jour de Merci Donnant was first started by a group of Pilgrims (Pèlerins) who fled from l'Angleterre before the McCarran Act to found a colony in the New World (le Nouveau Monde) where they could shoot Indians (les Peaux-Rouges) and eat turkey (dinde) to their heart's content.

They landed at a place called Plymouth (now a famous voiture Américaine) in a wooden sailing ship called the Mayflower (or Fleur de Mai) in 1620. But while the Pèlerins were killing the dindes, the Peaux-Rouges were killing the Pèlerins, and there were several hard winters ahead for both of them. The only way the Peaux-Rouges helped the Pèlerins was when they taught them to grow corn (maïs). The reason they did this was because they liked corn with their Pèlerins.

In 1623, after another harsh year, the Pèlerins' crops were so good that they decided to have a celebration and give thanks because more maïs was raised by the Pèlerins than Pèlerins were killed by Peaux-Rouges.

Every year on the Jour de Merci Donnant, parents tell their children an amusing story about the first celebration.

It concerns a brave capitaine named Miles Standish (known in France as Kilomètres Deboutish) and a young, shy lieutenant named Jean Alden. Both of them were in love with a flower of Plymouth called Priscilla Mullens (no translation). The vieux capitaine said to the jeune lieutenant:

"Go to the damsel Priscilla (allez très vite chez Priscilla), the loveliest maiden of Plymouth (la plus jolie demoiselle de Plymouth). Say that a blunt old captain, a man not of words but of action (un vieux Fanfan la Tulipe), offers his hand and his heart, the hand and heart of a soldier. Not in these words, you know, but this, in short, is my meaning.

"I am a maker of war (je suis un fabricant de la guerre) and not a maker of phrases. You, bred as a scholar (vous, qui êtes pain comme un étudiant), can say it in elegant language, such as you read in your books of the pleadings and wooings of lovers, such as you think best adapted to win the heart of the maiden."

Although Jean was fit to be tied (convenable à être emballé), friendship prevailed over love and he went to his duty. But instead of using elegant language, he blurted out his mission. Priscilla was muted with amazement and sorrow (rendue muette par l'étonnement et la tristesse).

At length she exclaimed, interrupting the ominous silence: "If the great captain of Plymouth is so very eager to wed me, why does he not come himself and take the trouble to woo me?" (Où est-il, le vieux Kilomètres? Pourquoi ne vient-il pas auprès de moi pour tenter sa chance?)

Jean said that Kilomètres Deboutish was very busy and didn't have time for those things. He staggered on, telling what a wonderful husband Kilomètres would make. Finally Priscilla arched her eyebrows and said in a tremulous voice, "Why don't you speak for yourself, Jean?" (Chacun à son goût.)

And so, on the fourth Thursday in November, American families sit down at a large table brimming with tasty dishes, and for the only time during the year eat better than the French do.

No one can deny that le Jour de Merci Donnant is a grande fête and no matter how well fed American families are, they never forget to give thanks to Kilomètres Deboutish, who made this great day possible.

Reprinted with permission of the Art Buchwald estate

A bad beginning makes a bad ending.

Euripedes

Beginnings

A column fights for attention against neighboring headlines, stories, photos, and even clever ads. With a strong opening paragraph, the columnist aims to halt readers in mid-scan.

"Wait a minute, what's this about?"

Therefore, the lead should wear a mink coat and a Mao cap. It's the catalyst to interesting conversation. Odd. Provocative. Different. Suddenly, the reader wants to know more.

Before crafting your lead, first consider the overall message of your column, because your first four to six lines will be crucial. The opening lines should introduce your subject and the direction you are taking in way that will make the reader care about what happens next.

Therefore, it helps to know what you plan to talk about.

Award winning columnist Derrick Jackson of *The Boston Globe* suggested this exercise.

"Type the point of your column in one sentence without a comma. If you cannot write it in one sentence, then you are not ready to write," he said at a 2006 NSNC meeting in Boston.

As a condensed form of writing, the average 500- to 700-word column should spill its guts quickly. By comparison, a novel can allow one to three chapters to introduce its story and characters. In scriptwriting, the main players and plot are revealed within the first ten pages. Not so in a column — the lead paragraph must serve to shoot the story out of a cannon.

Columnist and author David Chartrand of Universal Press Syndicate advises writers to strike fast and hard.

"Quick — say something! Get to the point before the reader

gets bored. Readers get bored if they have to work very long — like five or six seconds — figuring out what your commentary is about.

"How you do this — a statistic, a quote, dialogue, typing all the letters backwards — is not as important as doing it," says Chartrand, who won top prize from the National Society of Newspaper Columnists in 2002.

One of journalism's great storytellers is Pete Hamill, who received the NSNC's 2005 Ernie Pyle Lifetime Achievement Award in Texas. At that meeting, Hamill suggested columnists take a cue from movies in creating an opening scene.

Write cinematically. Think of the lead as an opening shot of a movie, where atmosphere and characters come alive with both a camera's wide shots and close-ups. But instead of camera work, paint the story with words.

Long before movies existed, authors such as Charles Dickens wrote picturesque opening scenes. Examine literary master-pieces to see how different authors introduced their readers through sentence structure and language. A few of Hamill's favorite authors include Frank O'Connor, Anton Chekhov, Irwin Shaw, and Ernest Hemmingway, and he applies techniques from great fiction to column writing for:

■ Getting a character onstage
■ Presentation of a character
■ Entering the dilemma of a story

Here is a classic example of one of Hamill's opening paragraphs:

The slow and tedious processes of justice brought Bernhard Hugo Goetz last week to a fifth-floor courtroom at 111 Centre Street, and there, at least, the poor man was safe. Out in the great scary city, the demons of his imagination roamed freely; across the street, many of them were locked way in the cages of The Tombs. But here at the defense table, flanked by his lawyers, protected by a half-dozen armed court officers, the room itself separated by metal detectors from the anarchy of the city, Goetz looked almost serene.

Pete Hamill, *The Village Voice*, May 12, 1987
Excerpted from his book collection, *Piecework*.

Crafting a lead is different for each writer. It can be a whisper. It can be a shout. Maybe it opens with an eye-popping scene or shocking statistics. The tone can be solemn or hilarious. There are no rules, and if there are, many columnists successfully break them.

Evoking emotion from a reader is one common bond among award-winning columnists. A sampling of lead paragraphs shows how writers use different emotions to grab and hold onto a reader's attention:

Outrage

President Bush is reportedly annoyed that the Chinese are using so much petroleum. With the world's fastest-growing economy, China's oil consumption has soared to at least 6.5 million barrels a day, and its market for automobiles is growing. If the boom continues, the Chinese may eventually be somewhere in the neighborhood of the United States, which burns up about 20 million barrels a day. Who do those Chinese think they are — Americans?

Cynthia Tucker, *The Atlanta Journal Constitution,*
April 23, 2006

Curiosity

I don't mean to be an alarmist, but the signs are impossible to ignore. We're dealing with an epidemic today that is more virulent than any strain of bird flu. I'm talking about the death of common sense and humility. You may think I'm talking about Tom Cruise's claim that he was going to eat his wife's placenta, but that's small potatoes compared to what came out of Inglewood recently.

Steven Lopez, *Los Angeles Times*, April 19, 2005

Belonging

Toby Keith and I are roughly the same age and both feeling the effects of our lost youth. I am overweight and have the knees of an 80-year-old, but in the back of my mind, I think I can dunk a basketball or run a 5-minute mile.

Don McNay, *CHNI News Service*, July 6, 2006

Provocation

Doing his stations of the Katrina cross, President Bush went for breakfast with Mayor Ray Nagin at Betsy's Pancake House. As Mr. Bush tried to squeeze past some tightly placed tables, a waitress, Joyce Labruzzo, teased him, saying, "Mr. President, are you going to turn your back on me?"

Maureen Dowd, *New York Times News Service,*
August 30, 2006

Humor

First black and gold, now red and pink. My eyes are so starved for a variety of color that if I saw a rainbow, the shock might detach my retinas. Every year at this time, I am called upon to help some bewildered guy or guys figure out what to get those special women in their lives. I usually suggest real estate, but how romantic is a housing bubble?

Samantha Bennett, *Pittsburgh Post-Gazette*

Discomfort

I was browsing at a newsstand in Manhattan recently when I came across a magazine called Felon. It was the "Stop Snitchin'" issue, and the first letter to the editor began, "Yo, wassup Felon." Another letter was from "your nigga John-Jay," who was kind enough to write: "To my bitches, I love ya'll."

Bob Herbert, *New York Times News Service*

Shock

What Lydia Cala Loggins suffered through in 2001 was horrific. Police barged through the front door of the Hurst house she grew up in and found her brother, Joseph F. Cala II, standing naked over the corpse of their mother, Lydia Cala. He was eating her heart, police said.

Dave Lieber, *Fort Worth Star-Telegram*, June 11, 2006

Though dramatically different, each lead launches the column's central theme and direction. Each opening forces an emotional reaction that compels the reader to know more.

In contrast, beware of the empty-calorie opener that tells the audience nothing. Writing coach and columnist Jim Stasiowski has trained journalists for the American Press Institute, and offered an example of a go-nowhere opening line:

Roger Olsen leaned back in his chair, lit a cigarette and looked out over the city.

Such words take up valuable space, but fail to inform. Such sentences are not intriguing. Words should illustrate, not merely decorate, according to Stasiowski.

Also, beware of the boring lead. It plays to an empty house:

What we're going to talk about today is global terrorism, but before I get to that, let me say ...

Snore.

If writing a winning lead is your forte, please step forward.

Not so fast, buster.

Fight complacency. Columnists can get too comfortable with their own styles and fall into a predictable pattern, according to Stasiowski.

Shake things up. Try something new. A habit is a mistake. A change will surprise readers and can lend greater depth to your work. For example, use a different writing style occasionally.

A hard-hitting lead is Stasiowski's typical style and he recalled one night when the murder of a young girl changed his writing pattern. As a columnist and reporter for *The Columbian* in Vancouver, Washington, he was doing a second-day story about the crime. After talking to the victim's divorced parents, his usual kapow-style opening felt wrong for the piece. He decided to imitate the style of John Branton, also of *The Columbian*, whom he described as an "ace cops reporter."

That led to this type of opening:

Nothing ever turned out right for Wanda Turner*.

"This sentence was the pure statement of the story's central conflict. She was a bright, energetic, loving young woman who, despite the best of intentions, made bad choices in jobs and in men. Her former fiancé had stabbed her to death one morning in her apartment," explained Stasiowski.

After the story ran, Stasiowski's editor complimented him on his uncharacteristic lead and encouraged him to use the style more often.

Don't get stuck in a pattern, no matter how well it works for you. Ease your opening prose into that mink coat and Mao cap. Startling readers will make them talk...about you.

(* Name changed at request of author.)

Cleanly, sir, you went to the core of the matter. Using the purest kind of wit, a balance of belief and art, you with a curious nervous elegance laid bare the root of life, and put your finger on its beating heart.

James Kirkup, British poet

Telling the Story

That was a wowser of a lead. Now what? The reader wants to know more, but many columns fall flat shortly after a well-executed opening.

"More often that not, the problem is no middle or ending. It's like the person sat up all night thinking of a cute lead and stopped there. There is no follow-through. No transitions. No point," says Chartrand.

To have a story unfold and resolve in about 600 words is a heavy gauntlet to throw down, and again, special subject columns require their own unique treatments. A one-size-fits-all format cannot apply. It is not a matter of placing all the statistics at the top of the column, or featuring a certain number of quotes. Sweeping sentences or to-the-point accounts can be equally successful.

A terrific subject alone won't carry a column. Scandals and celebrities are attention-getters, but memorable columns can be about small and ordinary things. For example, *USA Today's* Craig Wilson wrote about his mother's Thanksgiving gravy in a way that shimmered in my mind for a long time. A topic doesn't make a story great, the storytelling does.

For example, many holiday columns are predictable. In looking for a new angle, I wrote about one Thanksgiving when my husband and I, newly relocated, were taken under the turkey wing of two gay men who tackled the entire menu from *Gourmet*

Magazine. It was a hilarious three-day labor of love on their part to feed four people. Happily, reader emails described it as "refreshing."

The goal is to make readers care about your column, and they will when the writing is entertaining and easy to follow. Column writing is like building a house — the blueprints may vary, but the foundation must be solid and the lines true. Excellent writing takes shape with time and the application of the right tools, such as focus, organization, imagery, and smooth transition.

Focus

Simply put, "focus" is the point the columnist wants to make, that is, the message of the column.

"Focus means finding an engaging way to bring the reader into your writing and making the reader want to stay there to see what happens next," says Bill Tammeus of the *Kansas City Star* in Missouri.

Remember, the lead paragraph has done the job of reeling in the reader with an intriguing fact, a sudden laugh, or the description of a strange scene. Now the reader is curious. But beware. Sometimes a subject can radiate in different directions, all of them interesting.

So stay on point.

"Oh, please," you might say, "how can I lose my way in just 600 words?"

Oh, it can happen, especially when the topic offers alluring side trips into Tangent Town or Digression City. This is the perfect time to describe your column in one sentence.

The Central Conflict

One common example of unfocused writing is when a writer shares interesting facts or observations, but fails to tell a story.

According to Stasiowski, the central conflict is a column's overall theme. Smaller conflicts are the building blocks to the main focus of the story. However, sidetracking the reader on supporting details can obscure the core story or dilute a column's true message.

I made this mistake when I wrote a column about my own embarrassing brushes with celebrities:

The Cringe of Celebrity Encounters
By Suzette Martinez Standring

This is a confession. My few celebrity encounters will make you cringe. Tongue-tied and star-struck, my best foot forward always ends up in my mouth. Take for example, my ever-so-brief meeting with Dave Barry.

There I was at the Erma Bombeck Writers Conference last March. After giving a hilarious keynote, Barry enjoyed a brew with his buddies that evening at the hotel bar. At a far-off table, I sat stargazing at Barry. That's when I read his lips.

"I'm going to the bathroom," he said to his friends.

Oh! He's going to walk right past my chair! This is my chance to waylay him.

For those unfamiliar with highway robbery or being ambushed by bandits, the word, "waylay" means to accost, intercept or buttonhole — my intent exactly toward one of the world's great humorists. In fact, I'll disarm him with my clever vocabulary thought I.

So as Barry got closer, I leaned forward in my chair, smiled up at him and said, "Hi, Dave, can I waylay you for a second?"

Disgust filled his face.

"You want to what me?" he asked.

The crowded bar was noisy and it took me a second to realize, he didn't hear the "WAY" part!

In the dim tavern, I went scarlet. My guppy mouth opened and closed, soundless with shock.

Meanwhile, the ten people at my table swooped down and peppered Barry with questions and comments. I bobbed outside the perimeter, shouting out my defense.

"Way! Way! I said waylay!"

Too late, he couldn't hear me. I was merely a madwoman spouting off nonsequiters.

That's one more celebrity disaster in my collection. I have a history, you see.

Three years ago I was a fundraiser volunteer and David Halberstam was the event's keynote speaker. The planning committee asked me to be his driver.

His fans hold sacred any one of his fifteen best-selling books. Halberstam is a Pulitzer Prize winning journalist and historian. In comparison, I ascribe Pluto getting eight-balled off the solar system to planetary size discrimination. I tried to beg off from driving duty.

Crazily, the committee thought Halberstam and I had something in common.

"You're a writer, too!" said the chairman.

"Of fluff! What if I get stuck in traffic with him? I can't keep up an intelligent façade for too long, " I protested.

They waved me off to the train station, where upon his arrival, I discovered Halberstam is very tall.

"You know it's a community event when you're picked up in a green Honda Civic," I joked as he sat crumpled up in my car.

Later, the worst part was driving him back to his hotel in a blinding rain with faulty wipers.

"You should get them fixed. You're losing 36 percent of your visibility," were his only words during the ride.

I took his quiet for calm despite his white knuckles on the dashboard. Maybe he was speechless with terror on that Noah's Ark night. And why wouldn't he be? I missed the freeway entrance three times.

(I was probably preoccupied with his 36 percent comment — how did he arrive at that percentage?)

My celebrity gaffes go back to when I was 19. My old boss, attorney George T. Davis, was a member of the San Francisco Host Committee, which was frothy with the cream of high society. Often they welcomed dignitaries and celebrity guests to the city.

One week, Thubten Norbu, the brother of the Dalai Lama, was in town and a welcome reception was planned. My boss and his wife invited me to tag along to the soiree.

At 19, I didn't know His Holiness, The 14th Dalai Lama, was the supreme leader of Tibetan Buddhism and the bodily manifestation of an enlightened being. At 19, I probably spelled his title the Dolly Llama and thought he was connected to Himalayan wool farming.

But meeting his brother sounded nice.

We arrived in a room that swished with silk and suits. (I bet I was wearing a miniskirt and platform shoes.) People greeted each other with air kisses and "Lovely evening, darling!"

I was introduced to Dr. Norbu, an elegant and courteous man. Suddenly space opened up around us and we stood together alone. He looked at me expectantly. What does one say to the sibling of a reincarnated bodhisattva?

"So...how's your brother?" I ventured.

"Fine," he said.

"Have you seen him lately?" I asked.

Mercifully, a tide of people washed in around him and closed me out.

Oh, save me from myself. I said that at 19 and sadly, it's still my mantra at 52.

Though reader response was favorable, this column did not live up to its full potential. In it, I shared my embarrassment, but failed to leave readers with a meaningful message, according to friend and longtime columnist Dave Lieber of the *Fort Worth Star-Telegram.*

Here is a summary of his suggestions:

You should have stopped with Dave Barry, which was your strongest story. It's very funny and could have stood on its own.

The extra stories watered it down and filled up space, which didn't give you room to teach the reader the lesson you learned from the "waylay."

Without a message, the column doesn't fly. If you didn't learn a lesson from your experience to share with readers that is meaningful, emotional, warm and funny, then you shouldn't write about it.

This was valuable advice he learned from his days with *The Philadelphia Inquirer.* Bless his heart for passing it on to me...and now to you.

A Reminder of Purpose

"Write a headline for a quick summary," suggested Laura Pulfer, formerly with the *Cincinnati Enquirer* and 1999 inductee into the Cincinnati Journalism Hall of Fame by the Society of Professional Journalists. To the attendees at the 2006 Erma Bombeck Writers' Workshop, Pulfer suggested the following questions when drafting a column:

■ What is the column's purpose?

■ How do you want the reader to feel?

■ What do you want the reader to remember most?

A column headline works as a handy reminder for staying on point and can be compared to the "logline" in scriptwriting. On a DVD's box, the logline contains the nutshell description of the movie, such as this example:

It's A Wonderful Life: No one is born to be a failure. No one is poor who has friends.

A logline is used to pitch a possible movie to producers, so a scriptwriter has to come up with a brief project summary, no matter how complex the plot.

Similarly, in column writing, a summary headline can keep a columnist in the center lane as he drives through a draft. Otherwise, the possible danger is weaving all over the page with readers later yelling, "Hey, buddy, which way are you going?"

As a novice columnist I once wrote about tattoos. Later, it became clear that I was unclear. Was my column about entering the corporate world branded with a barbed wire wristlet? Or was it about symbolism as seen through youthful eyes? Or was I writing about later regrets by the tattooed?

When my editor asked me, even I couldn't say. Thus, my introductory lesson to the importance of focus. My drafting process could have been speedier had I penned a summary caption: "Shock at seeing the sign of Capricorn inked between my daughter's shoulder blades."

Organization

Order your writing so that questions in a reader's mind are answered in a logical sequence. Readers demand a smooth ride, moving from point to point easily. They should not bump up against boulders ("Where did that come from?"), or get tangled in the rushes ("Who is she referring to now?") or feel a loss of control ("Where is this heading?").

In journalism, the writer seeks to answer each of the following questions:

Who — the identities of the main character(s)
What — the event, experience, or issue
When — date, time period, or chronology
Where — location
How — the cause, procedure, or instructions
Why — motive, reason, conclusion

If each of these questions is answered, the story is told.

Remember, the lead introduces an idea or a story. From there, each paragraph should build on the column's premise.

Make Every Word Count

Powerful storytelling uses precise description. For each line written, ask yourself, "What does this do to sharpen the focus of my column?" Mystery novels and columns share this in common: many words and phrases hold clues that point toward the ultimate conclusion. Apply a keen sense of observation to the storytelling.

A reader yearns to have a person or event come alive. First-hand witnessing by a writer can add the unique dimension of mannerisms, gestures, and habits of a character.

Here are two writing examples by McCarty, both from the *Dayton Daily News*, that show how telling details can be spare, but profoundly revealing:

Emily Goldman never met Sister Dorothy Stang. David Stang can't remember a single day of his life when he didn't feel the presence of his older sister, a gentle but determined soul gunned down last year in the Amazon rainforest. The 73-year-old Dayton-born nun recited the Beatitudes to her attackers.

The gregarious child greeted them with hand-written signs scrawled on the drywall all over her flood-damaged home: "Welcome friends!" Even more poignant is what group leader Sue Cox of Englewood found the morning after the volunteers installed new kitchen cabinets. Cox was puzzled by the bedsheets tucked neatly inside the cabinets, but Natalie soon solved the mystery. "I slept there last night," the girl said. "It was very dark, but I felt very safe."

Each description must serve a purpose. Avoid details that do not build on your column's blueprint.

"Don't tell people that the car was fire engine red unless it tells you something about that individual," McCarty told writers at a 2006 Erma Bombeck Writers Workshop.

Sprinkle Interesting details within each paragraph. They encourage the reader to stay put.

"Form follows function. Bury little nuggets of candy that bring the reader a little farther along," added Pulfer.

Don't Shut Readers Out

Being easily understood is vital. Do not presume everybody knows the background of a popular topic. A better presumption is a reader's unfamiliarity with the issues, the players, or the what-happened-after-that of a situation.

When writing about current events or a follow-up column to an ongoing issue, the writer should be considerate of readers who, for whatever reasons, are not "in the know." If readers feel excluded by language or references, the columnist loses a potential audience.

Updating readers requires no lengthy introduction, especially in widely covered events. Instead, offer an explanatory line or brief refresher note to help lost souls get their bearings. Also, clarification can be done through context, so keep a self-explanatory approach in mind.

Also, unfamiliar words turn readers off, such as slang, television references, and pop culture shorthand. If not clued in, readers may decide they cannot relate to you as a columnist. How can they focus on your message if they are stumped by the words you use?

Early in my newspaper career, I presumed everyone knew what I knew, and therefore, I was fond of using pop culture jargon. One editor nagged me into curbing this bad habit.

"Don't use those terms. Assume you're writing for my grandmother who never gets out," said Mr. Wright (Who-Is-Never-Wrong, as I secretly called him).

"Oh, come on! Everyone knows what it means. Why do I have to write with the lowest common denominator in mind?" I said.

(Obviously, both my writing and my mouth needed to mature).

But Mr. Wright-Who-Is-Never Wrong lived up to his name, and his sound advice carried over into my column writing. It's hard to believe, but many readers could draw a blank at "Bennifer," the once famous pairing of celebrities Jennifer Lopez and Ben Affleck. (See how that's done?)

Transition

Another valuable tool is the use of transition. It's a writer's "GPS," that is, a way to keep readers apprised of signposts and their own location within your column.

Graceful transition creates an effortless read. The writing goal is to seamlessly connect the beginning, the middle and the end. A column is personal in tone, sharing memories or opinions within a very limited space. Often a columnist can display mood swings, or a change of time frame, all within 700 words.

The reader must remain unconfused during these changes. Switching gears smoothly is called transition and certain words, such as "however," or "nevertheless" act as signposts akin to "Change Ahead."

I Read An Echo

Another transition technique is to either "foreshadow" in one paragraph what lies ahead in the next, or to begin a new paragraph by "echoing" thoughts from the previous one. Written with a subtle hand, such cross references reinforce a train of thought and can serve to ground the reader as new ideas are presented.

Jeff Jacoby of *The Boston Globe* uses this technique and says, "I've always tried to achieve forward momentum in a column by having each paragraph advance from the point where the previous one stopped."

He did this in his June 14, 2006 column, *Signs of Success in Iraq*. What follows are **only** the first sentences from his column's fourteen paragraphs. Notice how each sentence echoes the one before it, and yet each new paragraph offers new information.

When Iraq's Prime Minister Nouri-al-Maliki announced last week that a US airstrike had killed terrorist leader Abu Musab al-Zarqawi, Iraq reporters burst into cheers and applause.

Important and welcome as Zarqawi's assassination was, it didn't put a dent in the quagmire-of-the-week mindset that depicts the war as a fiasco wrapped in a scandal inside a failure.

Virtually from day one, the media have reported this war as a litany of gloom and doom.

Some of this defeatism was inevitable, given the journalistic predisposition for bad news.

But there have also been highly negative assessments of the war from observers who can't be accused of habitual naysaying or Bush-bashing.

Another thoughtful commentator, The Washington Post's David Ignatius, had been even more despairing one day earlier: "This is an Iraqi nightmare," he wrote, "and America seems powerless to stop it."

But not everyone is so hopeless.

In the June issue of Commentary, veteran Middle East journalist Amir Taheri describes "The Real Iraq" as a far more promising place than the horror show of conventional media.

What are those realities?

He begins with refugees.

A second indicator is the pilgrim traffic to the Shi'ite shrines in Karbala and Najaf.

A third sign: the value of the Iraqi dinar.

Finally, says Taheri, there is the willingness of Iraqis to speak their minds.

As Congress embarks on a wide-ranging Iraq debate this week, Taheri's essay is well worth reading.

Remember, only the first sentences of his new paragraphs are featured above. Note how the first word or beginning phrase signals a new thought or change by Jacoby, but "echoes" past references. The sentences operate like an outline, keeping both the writer and the reader focused. As a result, readers enjoy a smooth transition through a complex topic.

Readers love an easy ride, and in return, they reward their columnist with rapt attention.

Speak properly, and in as few words as you can, but always plainly; for the end of speech is not ostentation, but to be understood.

William Penn

Putting Endings First

By Christopher "Chip" Scanlan, The Poynter Institute
(This article first appeared on Poynter Online,
www.poynter.org)

The quote has become the default ending in American journalism and readers and writers are all poorer for it.

The other day I randomly picked some news websites, clicked on stories, and scrolled to the bottom. Try it yourself. Open a newspaper, pick a story, and let your eyes drift to the end. There they are, those disembodied voices that bring way too many news stories to a close.

Ending a story with a quote is a reflex action, understandable especially in the crush of deadline, but overused to the point of cliché. Worse, the kicker quote deprives writers and readers of other, more effective ways to make their stories memorable.

In the world of newswriting, leads get most of the attention, but endings are equally, if not more, important.

If leads are like "flashlights that shine down into the story," as *The New Yorker's* John McPhee once put it, endings can be eternal flames that keep a story alive in a reader's head and heart.

Anne Hull used a fact to convey the impact of a street crime on a woman police officer at the end of her three-part narrative series, "Metal to Bone" in the *St. Petersburg Times*:

Lisa rarely thinks of Eugene, although she refuses to leave her back exposed, even while having dinner at a restaurant. Her back is always against a wall.

Sam Stanton of the *Sacramento Bee* could have quoted any number of observers when he witnessed an execution in 1992, but he chose a declarative sentence — "After 25 years and nine days, California's gas chamber was back in operation" — to signal an end, and a new beginning.

"You can't have a decent story if it doesn't leave you with a strong feeling or sense of image," Rick Bragg told me when I interviewed him in 1995, the year he won both the Pulitzer Prize and the ASNE award for feature writing.

Bragg's Pulitzer Prize-winning package of stories offers an object lesson for writers and editors looking for different options for a story's ending.

Two stories end in quotes. A profile of the southern Sheriff who persuaded Susan Smith to confess that she drowned her two children and blamed a black man for the crime concludes with a comment from the cop: "Susan Smith is smart in every area," he said, "except life."

The story about an Alabama prison for elderly and disabled inmates ends with a comment about undertaking students at a local university who prepare prisoners' bodies for burial: "They make 'em up real nice," the warden said.

In a profile of a black Indian of Mardi Gras in New Orleans, Bragg certainly had the material to use the same device.

Mr. Bannock sits and sweats in his house, working day and night with his needle. He has never had time for a family. He lives for Fat Tuesday.

"I need my mornin' glory," he said.

Most writers would have ended the story there with that colorful quote, but Bragg chose a detail instead that struck the chord of his theme: one man's devotion to a tradition larger than himself.

A few years ago he had a heart attack but did not have time to die. He had 40 yards of velvet to cut and sew.

There are several reasons why when faced with a blank space at the end of a story, most reporters plug in a quote.

One is expediency; it's a quick and easy way to finish.

But there's another, subtler explanation that has to do with the process of reporting. Reporters often begin in the dark, uncertain about the meaning of the events or issues that they must chronicle or explain. At least once during this confusing journey, the reporter hears — or reads — something that produces a moment of sudden clarity.

The words jump off a page or emerge from a source's mouth and into the notebook or tape recorder, and suddenly the reporter grasps the meaning. The squawky violin plays a true note. The piece slides into the puzzle. All that's missing are the quote marks. And the very next thought is, "Whew! I've got my ending!"

That moment helps the reporter understand the story, but it doesn't have the same effect on the reader who hasn't come along on the same journey of discovery and who needs different kinds of information to satisfactorily complete the reading process.

"A good ending absolutely, positively, must do three things at a minimum," Bruce DeSilva of The Associated Press told participants at the 2001 Narrative Journalism Conference co-sponsored by the Nieman Foundation and Poynter:

■ Tell the reader the story is over.

■ Nail the central point of the story to the reader's mind.

■ Resonate. "You should hear it echoing in your head when you put the paper down, when you turn the page. It shouldn't just end and have a central point," DeSilva says. "It should stay with you and make you think a little bit. The very best endings do something in addition to that. They surprise you a little. There's a kind of twist to them that's unexpected. And yet when you think about it for a second, you realize it's exactly right.

In some cases, the writer just needs to reorganize. Take that kicker quote and move it up higher, to buttress a description, or punctuate a section. Find something else that reinforces the story's theme. Think harder about the ending, as Bob Baker does here.

Write the ending first, as Jon Franklin advises, so you'll have a destination to aim for. Or at least know what it is.

"My advice to young people is to know what your ending is before you start writing," Ken Fuson of the *Des Moines Register* says.

Whatever ending you choose, don't make it an afterthought. Very few readers will return to that brilliant lead you sweated over. The last thing they'll read, if you've done your job right, is the end. Make it count.

Several years ago, Jack Hart, the veteran editor, coach, and writing teacher, helped writers and editors see myriad possibilities for beginning a story with his "Lexicon of Leads."

In that spirit, I propose an Encyclopedia of Endings. Here are a few sample entries, drawn primarily from Don Murray.

Anecdotal ending

"The anecdote is a brief story," Murray says. "It combines character, place, dialogue, action, and reaction. It summarizes by implication and demonstration."

Detail ending

"The writer uses a specific detail, a concrete image, a fact, a statistic to conclude the story by implication. The part stands for the whole and allows the reader to take a specific piece of information away with him," Murray says.

Face ending

"This ending allows the writer to stand back and let the camera focus on a significant person in the story," Murray says. See detail ending.

Narrative quote ending

Most quotes in newspaper stories are contemporary, made usually in response to a reporter's questions, rather than narrative, those "made at the time of the events being described," a distinction James B. Stewart draws in "Follow the Story."

Quote ending

"A quotation in itself is a piece of information," Don Murray says. "Its authority comes from the speaker, not the reporter. It gives a sense of objectivity to the story, and it allows for a conclusion in a manner that the reader will accept and believe. It lets the writer get out of the way."

Scenic ending

"This ending allows the writer to stand back and let the reader see the story," Murray says.

Schwab ending

Columnist Tommy Tomlinson coined this name in honor of a *Charlotte Observer* editor named Gary Schwab who taught him to look for the unexpected ending.

In a story about a young fishing star who died in a plane crash, Tomlinson ended with a description of his family scattering his ashes. "That's the ending I expected," Schwab told the reporter. "Can you give me an ending I didn't expect?"

In the interview I conducted with him for the upcoming "Best Newspaper Writing 2004," Tomlinson described going back to his notes; he found a scene where the fisherman's parents were playing a video of their son the day he caught his first fish.

"When I put that down there, I thought, that is such a better ending to the story because it ... brings it back to the beginning, and it adds such a richness to what is going on not only in this kid's life but in his family life.

"Any time I have a big story like this, I try to think, 'Is there a Schwab ending that I could put on this story?'"

Christopher "Chip" Scanlan is senior faculty-writing and director, National Writers Workshops and journalism advisor, NewsU, The Poynter Institute.

The U.S. Constitution is less than a quarter the length of the owner's manual for a 1998 Toyota Camry, and yet it has managed to keep 300 million of the world's most unruly, passionate and energetic people safe, prosperous and free.

P.J. O'Rourke

Column Length

How long should a column be? A column can range from 250 to 1,000 words. Some may harrumph! their objection to word limitation given the unlimited storage space on the Internet. But knowing when to quit writing is key to developing publication-worthy skills. Adhering to limited newspaper space is a good discipline, and if you want to be published in print, then compact writing is essential.

Know your audience. Before making a column submission, read target publications to get a sense for content and length. Typically, column requirements are posted under submission guidelines on a newspaper's Web site. Or, contact an editor for the ideal word count for a column.

Length can be referred to in various terms. It can be measured by a straight word count, as in a "700-word column." Or sometimes a column is assigned a certain number of "inches," depending on needs and space limitations of a newspaper. For example, when I worked for the *Hunterdon County* (NJ) *Democrat*, the editor allowed me "thirteen inches" for my humor column on the editorial page.

Craig Wilson of *USA Today* writes a popular Life Section column, and he does not measure his column by word count or inches, but rather, as "one hundred sentences."

Whatever length has been allowed in the past, it is a fact that nowadays newspaper column space is shrinking. Exceptions to length limitations are blogs and columns posted on Web sites, (and we've all read Internet pieces that stretch out for miles).

Columnist Bill Tammeus of the *Kansas City Star* in Missouri has enjoyed 40 years in the business. Over time, he has observed a newspaper industry trend toward shorter columns.

"Ten or twenty years ago it wasn't unusual to find op/ed [opinion/editorial] columns in the 850 to 1,000 word range. Now 700 words is a rough max. Because papers are shrinking for many reasons, I'm sure editors would prefer 500-word columns, but some things can't be said in 500 words," says Tammeus, a former president of the National Society of Newspaper Columnists.

Column Inches

A newspaper page is laid out with spaced rows of vertical columns containing articles, ads, and graphics. A "column inch" equals one column wide x one inch high. Since a newspaper page can vary in overall width, a column's width will vary, too. Depending on the newspaper's page size, columns can number four, five, six, or eight across on a page.

Typically, a columnist will be allotted a certain amount of space, which might be guided by a word count, or "x" amount of column inches.

A column inch is typically about 40 words, but if an editor assigns you a column length and you're unsure, ask him for a specific word count.

Metro columnist Dave Lieber scrutinizes local politicians and questionable practices as "The Watchdog" for the *Fort-Worth Star Telegram* in Texas. His pieces average about 800 words, sometimes more, because his columns include in-depth studies and investigative reports.

Home Forum of the Christian Science Monitor asks for "upbeat, personal essays" within the range of 300 to 900 words.

Art Buchwald easily wrote 8,000 columns over his 55–year career as a political satirist. Most of his columns contained about 500 words.

Many humorists find 500 word columns to be ideal. Kristen Twedt of the *Hattiesburg American* in Mississippi offered a homespun take on Shakespeare's quote, "Brevity is the soul of wit" when she wrote:

"Rhythm, timing and conservative word counts dictate every column I produce. The challenge is always to get the laughs without inducing brain strain. Anything over 500 words proves to be too much of a commitment for lots of readers. I try to be sensitive to that."

On the practical side, a short column stands a greater chance of newspaper publication due to space limitations.

However, not all lengthy pieces are kicked into "the round file" automatically. A fresh angle is a sharp foot in the door. Editor L. Kim Tan of *The Boston Globe* has run 1,400-word columns when the perspective is unique and the topic timely.

"Typically, a column can be 800-900 words," he says.

When sticking a big toe into the pool of publication, wade in with a 500- to 600-word column. If it catches the eye of an editor, you may be invited to expand it. On the other hand, there's nothing worse than laboring over 1,500-word piece on evolution v. intelligent design, having it deemed brilliant by a major newspaper, then being told, "But it's too long and we don't have the space." That's what happened to a novice freelancer who cried on my shoulder.

"Well, why can't the editor just edit it down? Isn't that his job?" she asked.

Editors have plenty to do under deadline. Sometimes they don't want to spend time chiseling down the work of an unfamiliar writer. Chances are they have other submissions equally brilliant in a much shorter form.

Flexibility and an increased word count may follow when an editor trusts you. This familiarity happens over time, when the columnist exhibits proven talent and reliability.

But first you have to get the nod from an interested editor. As genius as your 1,800-word column on the parallels between mink farming and behavioral economics may be, cut it down. When it comes to newspaper space, size does matter.

Writing Tips From Two Columnists

Here, columnists Robert L. Haught and Oon Yeoh share their personal tips for column writing success.

The 4-S Formula

By Robert L. Haught
Washington Columnist, *The Oklahoman*

In my column-writing I try to follow a "4-S" formula:

■ Make it short — and by that I mean not too wordy. With an ever-shrinking news hole, that's not an option but a necessity.

■ Make it simple — don't insult the reader's intelligence, but if you want it to be read it has to be readable.

■ Make it sound — apply the principles of journalism ethics and make the column stand up to close scrutiny.

■ Make it sing — it's not enough to have a tightly-written, fact-based, easily-read piece, it must be powerful enough to compete with everything else that meets the reader's eye.

For someone who writes about the wacky world of Washington, D.C., brevity is a tough challenge. Verbosity rules on Capitol Hill — witness the inches-thick daily editions of the *Congressional Record*. The filibuster is an institutionalized practice of using as many words as possible to say nothing. The bureaucracy is a breeding ground for voluminous regulations and ponderous pronouncements.

Government officials tend to be tone deaf to the cry of "trim the fat," but a newspaper columnist has little choice. And I'd rather make my own cuts than have an editor do it. So when my newspaper had a radical redesign and dropped some columns, I willingly trimmed mine to 500 words.

Simplicity is equally difficult to achieve in the environment of

51

the nation's capital. Historically public administrators have had difficulty expressing their thoughts and ideas simply and clearly. A plain-talking Texan, Rep. Maury Maverick, put a label on the problem when in 1944 he coined the word "gobbledygook" to describe bloated, pompous, official language. He once told his staff: "Anyone using the words 'activate' or 'implement' will be shot."

My all-time favorite columnist, Will Rogers, set a good example for simple writing. Some of his most-quoted sayings use words of one or two syllables: *"I don't make jokes, I just watch government and report the facts." "No man is great if he thinks he is." "All I know is what I read in the papers."*

As a former UPI correspondent, I was taught to write for "the Kansas City milkman." In other words, make your writing easily understood by the average reader.

Among the all too many ethical violations by columnists in recent years is the brazen act of making up facts, fabricating quotes, and inventing characters. Since my "Potomac Junction" column frequently indulges in satire, I've had to be careful not to mislead the reader in writing about Congressman Babble and Senator Stump and the Congressional Hindsight Committee.

So often in Washington true stories are so absurdly unbelievable that it's advisable to copy Dave Barry and say in one way or another, "I'm not making this up."

As for making a column "sing" to get the reader's attention, that's where the writer's "voice," or distinctive style, is important. When I sit down at the keyboard I have to ask myself, "how can I make this column different from the others?" Here are some approaches that seem to have worked:

■ To illustrate the confusion over the new Medicare prescription drug plan, I did a takeoff on the old Abbott and Costello "who's on first" routine. I knew the reference to the Golden Days of Radio wouldn't connect with young people, but I doubt they read my stuff anyway.

■ Applying a humorous twist to a serious situation, when O. J. Simpson was accused of murdering his wife, I speculated on how that might impact a lobbyist for the orange juice industry.

■ My lead for a roundup of Yuletide humor was inspired by a real news item: "You know the Christmas season is here when the Washington-Baltimore Bare Buns Family Nudist Club kicks off its annual holiday clothing drive."

■ For a 1998 Thanksgiving column, I envisioned Philanderer-in-Chief Bill Clinton performing public service by manning the Agriculture Department's poultry hotline.

Q: How do you thaw a turkey?

A: My best advice ... is that you stretch it out as long as you can, all the while denying that the problem exists.

I've learned that most readers can go along with a whimsical joke — they've offered suggestions for a Smokey the Bear for President campaign and sent grocery discount coupons to help a president and first lady burdened with legal bills. Others take ridicule too seriously, as when I wrote about a defeated Al Gore putting on a few pounds. Some accused me of defaming fat people.

The "4-S" formula for writing might not work for everybody. But since my column has been running since 1989, I've concluded I must be doing something right.

10 Tips

By Oon Yeoh
Columnist, *Today* (Singapore)

1. Write with conviction: Put forward your opinion as something you truly believe in. Argue your case with conviction. Come down hard on one side of an issue. Be unequivocal. Never ever sit on the fence.

2. Maintain your focus: Make your column about one thing and one thing alone. Don't muddle the message. Maintain your focus. That's the only way to make a strong impression on your readers and to convince them that your point of view is correct.

3. Understand opposing viewpoints: Be mindful of the opposing argument. Anticipate objections to your point of view and deal with them convincingly with sound reasoning. If you're not familiar with the opposing view, you will not be able to argue your points well.

4. Refer to facts: Your arguments, however logical, will not carry much weight unless they are accompanied by facts that support your position. Don't overdo this and inundate your readers with statistics and figures. But do make use of facts from reputable sources.

5. Use analogies: Analogies are useful for illustrating a point, especially when the topic you are writing about is somewhat complicated or technical. Using a simple analogy from everyday life makes the issue more understandable and relevant to the reader.

6. Be critical: People like reading columnists who dare to criticize real life people — not just nameless concepts and policies. Naming names might create a bit of controversy, but as long as you do not libel anyone and don't go overboard in your criticism, it works well to make your column an interesting and exciting read.

7. Do reporting: It's possible to write columns without doing any reporting, but the best columns typically involve some form of reporting. When you report, you get on the ground and you gain a better sense of what's really happening. When you write from an ivory tower, it shows.

8. Localize and personalize: Localize your story whenever possible. Also tie it to some personal experience — yours or that of someone you know. This makes an otherwise esoteric and distant topic more real, relevant, and memorable to the reader.

9. Be passionate: Generally, people don't like to hear a soft or passive voice when they read a column. So be aggressive — even arrogant, to an extent. People want to see passion. They want to feel energized. If the issue doesn't seem to excite you, the writer, it's certainly not going to excite the reader.

10. Provide a solution: Last but not least, don't just raise an issue. Have the conviction to suggest a solution. Columns that criticize certain policies but offer no solutions are useless. People read columns because they want to gain insight and answers. If you don't provide those, you've failed as a columnist.

Excerpted with permission from *Column Writing Tips* by Oon Yeoh, oonyeoh.squarespace.com

Writing is fighting.

Muhammad Ali

The Big, Bad, Blank Screen

Blink. Blink. Still Blank. The clock ticks and an editor's foot goes a'tapping. At some point, a columnist struggles with writer's block. Meeting every deadline requires leading a new charge. Some days, it's a spunky ride to the top of Victory Hill. Other days, it's trek through the mud, regroup and attack from another angle.

Even the most seasoned columnists wring their hands, as if trying to squeeze a column onto the keyboard. Often the undone column is due to time gobbled up with breaking news and other assignments, but there are days when the idea tank runs low and there I am bare mind to blank screen. An imaginary schoolmarm stands ready with a willow switch to rap my knuckles.

"You'll never make deadline. Get going, sister."

I timidly tap out a few lines. Suddenly, evil little elves whisper in my ear.

"Now that was stupid." "No way, man!" "You've got to be kidding me." "Oh, please..."

In pop psychology terms, meet my inner saboteurs.

Diversion

As a humor columnist, I meet their disruption with diversion.

I pen a pretend letter to a friend. Instead of writing for the invisible, hypercritical "them," I write to one good friend about a funny subject. It's the same trick professional speakers employ when they search out a friendly face in the audience when delivering a talk.

Since humor is spontaneous, this focus puts me in a relaxed storytelling mode. My comic timing and imagery improve when I'm not being self-censored at every keyboard tap. A draft gets developed.

Done. I cut and paste the best sections of my "letter" into a column, now ready for editing. In addition to a draft, I can mail off an actual letter to my friend. This appeals to my multi-tasking personality.

I smugly wink at my now-silenced hobgoblins. But make no mistake, they'll be back tomorrow.

How do other columnists cope?

Some colleagues say deadlines and job loss make good cattle prods. Others claim they "just sit down and do it." But many more conjure up a column with a trick or two of their own.

Take Notes

"Carry a notebook and write down ideas and thoughts and words as they come to you. You think you'll remember later, but you won't. I have lost hundreds of insights because I thought I'd remember," says Ellen Goodman of *The Boston Globe.*

Music Inspires

Tony Norman, metro columnist with *The Pittsburgh Post-Gazette* (PA) plays music that fits the mood of the column he wants to write.

"The best way to get your voice across in a column is to write quickly and audaciously. Today I'm listening to 'The Essential Bruce Springsteen' anthology because I'm writing about the liberal talk radio network. I needed something bombastic and funny and occasionally profound to stir up corresponding feelings that can be exploited on deadline," says Norman.

Role models and music inspire "Watchdog" columnist Dave Lieber of the *Fort Worth Star Telegram.*

"To help me get in the writing mood, I read an old column by Jimmy Breslin. He invented the modern metro news column. Or I might read a column by Steve Lopez of *The Los Angeles Times.* Then I sit down, in the right frame of mind, and let 'er rip! Music that fits that day's column is always playing in the background, usually the same song on repeat mode," he says.

Invite Disaster

If column material is M.I.A., go out and bring it back alive, according to Melissa Jarvis of *The Courier Post.*

"I will subconsciously invite disaster (and inspiration!) by creating a situation. I'll let my kids have five friends over and I'll get enough column material to get me out of my temporary slump," says Jarvis, who writes *The Family Album.*

Tim Bete, director of the Erma Bombeck Writers' Workshop, agrees.

"Go to the grocery store, fill your cart with 50 cans of Spam and a two-liter bottle of Mountain Dew. Go to the 12-Items-Or-Less checkout lane. Something funny will happen, I guarantee it," says Bete, a parenting humor columnist.

Scan Headlines

Satirist Art Buchwald credited politicians for making his job easy, sometimes too easy. For column fodder, he simply read the morning's headlines.

"Give me a Tom DeLay and I've got two columns. Give me Donald Rumsfeld and I get the day off," said Buchwald.

Others peruse the papers for easily overlooked gems.

Craig Wilson of *USA Today* says, "I scan papers every day, looking for one sentence, like 'People in Dayton are shoving jelly beans up their noses,' and I think, 'Oh, that's odd, maybe I can muse on that for 100 sentences.' "

Study the Enemy

Ernesto Portillo, Jr., a metro columnist for the *Arizona Star Daily*, reviews the work of opponents.

"If I'm writing a political column, I'll read the columns of other writers who approach the subject opposite to what I intend to write. I hone my arguments and logic by reading the polar opposite. I use direct, simple-to-the-point observations," says Portillo.

Get Mad

Outrage juices up Stu Bykofsky of the *Philadelphia Daily News*, who says, "Since my column has 'no limits,' I can draw inspiration from anything, paying particular attention to anything that pisses me off, or anything I see as an injustice. I also want to explain things to my readers, about how and why things happen in entertainment and politics — and there's almost always money involved."

Enlist Readers

One items columnist keeps an ear to the ground for tips and comments from readers. Smiley Anders pens a column six days a week for *The Advocate* in Baton Rouge, LA.

"Readers are quick to respond and keep things moving along. With 50 to 100 or more responses a day (e-mail, fax, snail mail, phone, scrawls on wet cocktail napkins, etc.), I can pick and choose items to get some variety. Years ago, a reader asked me, 'Don't you feel guilty getting paid for a column that other people write?' My response was no," says Anders, a five-time winner of the NSNC's Herb Caen Award.

Be Spartan

Be alone, cold, and hungry when inviting the muse. *Editor & Publisher* magazine's Dave Astor — who writes a freelance humor/satire column for *The Montclair* (N.J.) *Times* — thinks of ideas for his *Montclairvoyant* column on the train to and from his day job, and carries no other reading materials to avoid distraction.

"Then, when I write the column at home, I keep the thermostat down to stay as alert as possible. Also, I try not to eat much before writing because being hungry puts me in an edgier mood that helps in writing a satirical feature," says Astor.

Food Bribes and Stream of Consciousness

Chocolate ice cream with syrup and a steaming cup of coffee stave off writer's block for *Smile-Breaks* columnist Sheila Buska in Southern California. Her writing ritual includes a comfy chair, yellow-lined paper, and a favorite pen.

"I just keep talking to myself on paper until something falls out. Also, I take note of every frustration or irony I meet up with during the week and 'file it' for future columns," says Buska.

Waist Deep in Research

When creating a column for *Suddenly Senior,* Frank Kaiser surrounds himself with research materials, and "gets lost in the process."

"I spend hours separating the good stuff from the blow, and more hours calling and confirming facts and quotes. Finally, I sort it all out at the computer, forcing everything into a column of facts, insights and a bit of fun on what is, hopefully, an interesting subject to my age 50+ readers," says Kaiser.

Get Moving

Ellen Goodman of the *Boston Globe* says, "You can be good or bad, you just can't be late. If I'm feeling stuck or stressed or just trying to loosen up:

■ I read. Reading is like eating. It's food for the writer.

■ I walk around, and around, and around. I find the rhythm of my feet gets the brain going."

Escape and Reach Within

Tracey O'Shaughnessy with the *Republican American* (CT) believes writer's block is laziness. Bike, run, rake leaves, but don't just riffle through notes. Escape provides a way to reach within.

"The world is rich with wonder and with injustice. Look for it. Find it. Itch to scratch it. When the world is too dreary and dark for you, reach back into the well of your own memories. You may think they are dull and ordinary, but they are rich and unique and yours. All escape brings you back to who you are and what you are about," says O'Shaughnessey.

A Touch of Vice

Political columnist Phil Reisman of *The Journal News* (NY) gets started by pacing. After bothering newsroom colleagues and being told to go away, he takes long walks, sometimes driving to a wooden pier on Long Island Sound.

"I think about jumping in. Either the shock of the water will unclog my writer's block, or I'll drown. I drink black coffee, and I keep drinking it until I'm on such a caffeine jag that I'm practically bouncing off the walls. Not until then am I ready to write the column," says Reisman, who adds, "At least I don't smoke."

Sit Down and Do It

Christopher Kenneally, freelance columnist and director of author and creator relations for Copyright Clearance Center, simply gets to work, no tricks needed anymore. Ah, but to remember the days of smoke-filled newsrooms.

"I would have said to have four things easily at hand: cigarettes, matches, an ashtray, and white-out. At the dawn of the 21st century, I'm smokeless and paperless like most of us, but no great ritual has replaced that sublime old routine," says Kenneally, author of the book *Massachusetts 101*.

Syndicated columnist Marguerite Kelly of the *Washington Post* also needs no inner prodding.

"I remember the words from the late Edmond LeBreton, once head of the press gallery on Capitol Hill, who told me to 'put the seat of my pants to the seat of my chair,' and that's what I still do," says Kelly.

If you steal from one author, it's plagiarism; if you steal from many, it's research.

On Copyright

The following article is by Christopher Kenneally, director of author and creator relations for the not-for-profit Copyright Clearance Center. It first appeared in www.beyondthebook.com, *a resource on writing and publishing from CCC. Reprint permission granted.*

This article comes with its own warning, which is simply a reminder of what Mark Twain observed in the late 19th Century: "Only one thing is impossible for God — to find any sense in any copyright law on the planet. Whenever a copyright law is to be made or altered, then the idiots assemble."

Well, even Twain occasionally misspoke. It must be conceded that the Founders who wrote the Constitution of the United States were hardly "idiots." They chose, after all, to include a provision for copyright protection directly into that august document.

"The Congress shall have the power," states Article I, section 8, Clause 8, "...to promote the progress of science and useful arts, by securing for limited times to authors and inventors the exclusive right to their respective writing and discoveries." At the very first session of Congress, legislators passed the Copyright Act of 1790, which provided for a copyright protection term of 14 years, renewable for another 14.

Times change, and the copyright laws have regularly done likewise. Today, copyright protects a work for the lifetime of its "author" plus 70 years, and registration of that copyright in the

U.S. Copyright Office (itself an arm of the Library of Congress) opens the door to the courts for the copyright holder to sue an infringer. If the work was "made for hire," then the employer of the writer is considered "author" and a corporate "author" receives a copyright term of 95 years.

In other words, a hit song written in 2003 by a self-employed 20-year-old will remain protected by copyright in the United States until 2128 (if the writer lives to 75). However if that writer was an employee, then his employer's copyright would expire in 2098 no matter when the writer expired.

For all types of writers, the basics of copyright law are always worth bearing in mind. This is true especially if the writer is a freelance journalist or columnist and dreams of syndication or publishing a collection of his or her work.

What follows, then is a (highly subjective) round-up of a dozen tips for U.S. copyright consciousness:

1) From the moment any expression is fixed in form (written word and painted canvas are two traditional examples, but an electronic word processing file is considered "fixed" too), that work is immediately and automatically protected by copyright under U.S. and foreign law.

2) To be able to bring a suit against an infringer, however, does require having registered the copyright with the U.S. Copyright Office (www.copyright.gov), for which a $45 fee is currently charged. Please note that, if you are a self-employed freelance journalist, the copyright registration on the newspaper in which the article is published will likely not protect your own work.

3) As an incentive for registering copyright, the law provides that attorney's fees as well as statutory damages (which, in cases where "actual damages" are too hard to prove, can rise as high as $150,000 per infringement) may be paid in any successful court action for infringement if the registration occurred before the infringement.

4) A person's name or the name of a product "brand" cannot be protected by copyright law, although these may be protected by trademark law. For more information, contact the U.S. Patent & Trademark Office (www.uispto.gov).

5) Copyright ownership is not limited solely to the creators of works. For example, a writer may sign either a "Work For Hire" contract or an "All Rights" contract with a publisher or syndi-

cate. In the first case, the employer is the "author" for purposes of copyright right from the beginning and the writer has no rights; in the latter, the original author initially holds copyright rights and transfers them to another person (but matters like the length of copyright term continue to be measured by the original author's life.)

6) On the other hand, a publisher or syndicate does not automatically acquire copyright simply by publishing material. Unless there is a signed contract to the contrary, the original author retains copyright ownership and the publisher or syndicate acquires only a license.

7) Newspaper columnists, who may occasionally wish to reprint excerpts of another writer's work, should generally be free to do so. Section 107 of the U.S. Copyright Act allows for certain limited republication of copyrighted materials under what is known as "Fair Use." There is no specified amount of material that may be quoted without fear of infringement, though for a typical 600-word newspaper column, any such charge would likely seem exaggerated. Section 107 allows re-use without the copyright holder's permission, according to the U.S. Copyright Office (www.copyright.gov), "for quotation of excerpts in a review or criticism for purposes of illustration or comment; quotation of short passages in a scholarly or technical work, for illustration or clarification of the author's observations; use in a parody of some of the content of the work parodied; [and] summary of an address or article, with brief quotations, in a news report."

8) A copyright holder may license specific forms of re-use to a variety of publishers or others. Such re-uses may include film rights, foreign language rights, and merchandising rights (e.g., action figures in the shape of a comic strip character.)

9) Contrary to the opinion of most teenagers, a Web site (in whole or in part) is almost always protected by copyright. This applies not only to text, but also to photos and illustrations.

10) Unlike Web content, however, a domain name (e.g., www.beyond thebook.com) is not subject to copyright law. The Internet Corporation for Assigned Names and Numbers (ICANN) is responsible for overseeing the domain name system. Domain names can be registered for a fee with a variety of designated vendors, which are listed at www.icanno.org. In addition, the

ICANN Web site provides information about resolving domain name disputes.

11) When copyright issues arise between writers and publishers, a variety of writer's organizations may be able to provide assistance through their contract dispute resolutions programs, including The American Society of Journalists and Authors (www.asja.org); the National Writers Union (www.nwu.org); and the Authors Guild (www.authorguild.org)

12) Finally, because the law can change almost as often as Madonna's hair color, and is open to nearly as much interpretation as a Florida presidential election ballot, trust THIS advice most: always verify the currency and accuracy of any amateur copyright advice that you may receive with your editor, agent or attorney.

No passion in the world is equal to the passion to alter someone else's draft.

Working With Editors

The editor is not the enemy (it only feels that way sometimes). "Writers need editors to get the product to the marketplace. Ultimately, the editor and the publisher put the paper out. You have to live with editing. It's a fact of life," says L. Kim Tan, an editor with the *Boston Globe*.

If you're a new hire in the newsroom, listen and learn. If you are a freelance columnist and have just snagged space on a page, get acclimated to the newspaper's style. Trust between an editor and writer takes time, so be open to an editor's suggestions.

"The young have a duty to listen. You don't come up to a newspaper at age 23 fully formed. You're not. You'll be doing this the rest of your life," said lifetime award winner Pete Hamill in 2005 at a NSNC conference.

In 1998, at the age of 44 at my first newspaper job, I found newsroom training gives an employee something a freelancer doesn't get easily — a daily drubbing on what a writer does wrong. The stress to "put the paper to bed" under deadline can be hair-raising, so an editor's comments can be curt and to the point, if they are offered at all.

New to boot camp, it stung to be told by an editor to "tighten it up," or to "stick to one point," or even, "what's your point?" The wholesale relocation of my paragraphs was infuriating. Regarding correct attribution, I wanted to bash my keyboard over one editor's head if he yelled, "Sez who?!" one more time at me in front of the entire newsroom.

65

Still, such advice vastly improved my later work. An editor's job is to make content read better and revisions are not an indictment of one's ability.

Arianna Huffington shared her thoughts about editing at a 2006 NSNC conference in Boston. A syndicated columnist with Tribune Media Services, she is an author, TV host, and co-founder of www.huffingtonpost.com.

During her early years as a columnist, Huffington resisted editing.

"I know that at first I used to hate being edited because I took it as a personal insult, as a proof that I was really no good," said Huffington, "Then the more secure I grew, the more I started loving being edited, because I felt that I could take more risks and somebody would be there to catch me if I went too far, or if it didn't work."

What do editors want when working with columnists?

L. Kim Tan is one of two editors for the twice-weekly *Globe South*, a 16-page section of the *Boston Globe*, which covers the South Shore region of Massachusetts. Formerly, Tan founded a student newspaper while serving as assistant professor at Nanyang Technological University in Singapore. Sometimes he wishes writers could swap jobs with him because developing a dual mindset is helpful.

"It's true you want a reporter to think like an editor and an editor to think like a reporter," he says.

If a column needs revisions, often Tan will return the work with suggestions, or if needed, instructions for a redo. He feels it best if the writers perform the rewrite themselves in order to preserve the character of their writing and pride of ownership in the work.

"Writing doesn't give the financial payoff writers want, so I like to give them as much of their voice and style as possible," he says.

Freelancers sometimes send unsolicited work to him. Tan shared his selection process:

"First, we're looking at the writer — have we dealt with them before, or read anything by them before, or know anyone who has used them before? Can we get a quick reference from someone else?"

Tan finds there is potential when the writing:
- Is outstanding
- Is accurate with details
- Is easy to understand
- Evokes empathy

A diversity of voices and topics interest Tan since his section, *Globe South*, covers a large region. He looks for an article or column that "fills a hole," or "fills a need" not met by his staff.

Here, the *Boston Globe* editor answered questions about working with new writers.

Q: *Will a lengthy piece disqualify a writer from consideration?*

A: For Tan, length is dependent on the subject and scope. Generally, a piece can be 800-900 words, but a 1,400 word piece might be acceptable if the subject or writer's perspective is unique, or the story is interesting or substantive.

Q: *Will he work with previously unpublished writers?*

A: Tan reviews an unsolicited submission more as a basis for ability of a new writer.

"Sometimes we get someone really green. We always look at what they have to offer. I might ask for a couple of samples that were not published elsewhere. I want to see the quality, what they are capable of and then I'll ask for something different," he says, "Use what you've got to get more stuff to do."

Q: *Do writers with difficult personalities reduce their chances of getting published?*

A: "Sometimes the writer may be difficult but if the quality of work is high, it might be worth it. When it comes to freelancing, you must market yourself with quality writing and the ability to meet the editor's needs. It helps if you are cooperative and agreeable. If you can do both, you'll always get the job ahead of someone who can only do one," says Tan.

Q: *What if the writer objects to an editor's changes?*

A: It depends, according to Tan. In general, it's a cooperative relationship. The editor ultimately is responsible for what is published, but that is not to say writers shouldn't stand up for their work — especially if it's an opinion column and the writer and editor disagree over an issue.

(Note: Columnists are given more editorial leeway since a column reflects personal views. In comparison, news reporting must be objective and the writer is not allowed to insert him/herself into the story.)

"You don't have to give up your principles. If the editor wants to change your column to give it a different slant than what you intended, then as a columnist, it is incumbent upon you to say, 'No, this is not what I want.' Editing is trying to get the essence of what the writer is trying to convey," says Tan.

Q: *What is the best way to pitch a writing idea?*

A: "Can you describe your column in one sentence? If you can do that, then it can be made to work," he says.

Lisa McManus is another editor with a long career of working with columnists. *The Patriot Ledger* is a daily newspaper that serves 26 towns and cities south of Boston. McManus worked as a features editor for five of her 12 years with the paper. During that time she edited various sections, such as lifestyle, religion, home, health, entertainment, and food, and worked with a number of both staff and freelance columnists.

McManus believes the best relationship between columnist and editor is interactive and trusting. Her job is to keep a writer on track and to perform quality control over each piece.

"As an editor, I recognize that it's your voice, your opinion, your column, but it's in my section of the newspaper and the buck stops here. A columnist has to be open to constructive criticism, even if the editor has to say, 'It doesn't work, start over.'"

When there is a disagreement over edits, McManus suggests a series of frank and non-confrontational discussions between columnist and editor. The goal should be to establish trust and a good working relationship.

But if a truly bad match exists between writer and editor, perhaps it may be necessary to ask a supervising third party to mediate mutual goals. However, talks should take place first between columnist and editor before going up the chain of command. At times, both parties might not find resolution.

"If nothing can be done and someone is butchering your column, week after week, then walk," says McManus.

However, before quitting, she suggested a reality check.

Take copies of your columns, both before and after editing, to a trusted neutral party, someone who will tell you the truth. Perhaps perceived "butchering" is simply "thorough editing," and the revised column may be better.

"Some people just lack the perspective a good editor provides," McManus says.

What Do Editors Hate?

■ The adversarial columnist who can't take criticism.

■ Problems with meeting deadlines — this includes late submissions, requests for time extensions, or never writing in advance of vacations or emergencies. The gravest offense is to come up empty on deadline.

"It's very disappointing to readers and that's the worst thing you can do to them," says McManus.

■ The one-note column — be fresh in subject and approach.

■ Writing outside of the definition of an assigned column — this happens when a columnist's life changes or when interest is lost in the original topic; for example, the parenting columnist whose kids have left the nest.

■ The too-generic columnist who lacks a clear voice/style.

■ The column in need of universal appeal.

■ Columns that are written more in the style of journal or blog entries.

■ Columnists who cannot write to the assigned length — McManus says, "They expect me to cut it down. Most editors are multi-tasking and overburdened."

Getting an Editor's Attention

How can a columnist interest an editor in potential work? McManus offers these suggestions:

■ Before seeking a slot, be realistic about the time commitment involved. Do you have the ability to make a monthly, or weekly, or a three-times-a-week deadline?

■ A query letter should include information about yourself, the type of column you write and a list of ideas you'd like to pursue in your column.

■ Call up an editor and ask to submit samples.

■ Try a fresh approach. Pitch your column in a way that's different from other columns about the same subject. Explain your column in one to two sentences and suggest why it would increase readership.

■ Submit published column samples or offer at least four, full-length, publishable columns. These samples will give an editor a sense of your ability to produce and a good overview of your writing.

■ A universal theme is desirable.

■ Convey one idea within each column.

■ Offer your work to a small paper — try weeklies — and work your way up to bigger ones.

■ If you write a blog as a way to get a column, then write it in the style of a print column. Sprawling, unfocused writing is a turnoff to editors.

Expect to hear a lot of "no thanks" from editors whose budgets are squeezed beyond belief, but feel free to periodically check back and follow up because things can change.

Ego Management

Vanity, vanity, thy name is Writer.

I've met other columnists who insist that not one word, not one comma be changed. (Hard slap on the table for emphasis!) They argue a column is a personal reflection and as such, it should be left in its original form.

Some editors will bow to such demands, but only to their most experienced columnists, those with proven accuracy and writing skill. But since the best need the least amount of editing, perhaps it's not that much of a concession.

I am not a member of the elite Never Edited Club, although I've entered the Lightly Revised Association. Like other writers, I struggle between attachment to my prose and my desire to improve. If the meaning of an edited column remains unchanged, then I can hold my tongue, and many colleagues agree.

Tongue. Now there was a very bad edit. It still ruffles me to remember one long ago edit to my column about a personal cooking disaster. I had written, "I blew my toque!"

A toque is a chef's hat, but without checking with me first, the editor changed it to, "I blew my tongue!"

Oh, well, *usually* more good comes out of editing than not.

Before a diamond shows its brilliancy and prismatic colors it has to stand a good deal of cutting and smoothing.

Author Unknown

Self-Editing: Your Machete or Mine?

Editing one's own work serves two purposes. A writer exerts more control over the product and editors prefer ready-to-run work.

However, some writers are so attached to their prose, self-editing feels like self-mutilation. Yes, it hurts to "kill your darlings," as Mark Twain once called it, but sadly, some of them must go. Newspaper space is limited.

Lean writing attractively shapes the printed personality, so think of self-editing as dropping 50 pounds. Folks would say, "Aha! So that's what you really look like."

For 20 years, columnist Beverly Beckham wrote for *The Boston Herald* before moving to *The Boston Globe* in 2006. At her busiest, she wrote three lifestyle columns a week and just as many editorials.

"Writing is like whittling. You have to keep trimming and cutting until all you have left is all you need. Keep it simple."

Shimmering in the radiance of all the dawning splendor of the earth, the trees rocked to and fro, keeping rhythm with the lull of the breeze.

"I wrote this when I was in high school. I should have written, *a breeze blew and trees shimmered,*" says Beckham.

Can one clear-cut a story from 1,200 words to half its size and still offer a well-told tale? In 2005, I wrote about witnessing my granddaughter's birth, from first contraction to the baby's delivery, in 550 words. It can be done.

Craig Wilson of *USA Today* believes a shortened column will result in better details and satisfied readers.

"Your 600-word column will be better than your 1,000-word column because you only use your best stuff. Otherwise, it's too overwritten. Who can finish it?" he says.

Refining Under Deadline

"Deadline-driven journalists spend very little time refining their work. And that work often is compelling when written with passion and haste," says Mike Leonard of *The Herald Times* in Bloomington, Indiana.

But Leonard warns that later come the "improvement regrets" — a better synonym, the missing transition. Factor in time for buffing and polishing. Don't con yourself into blaming deadlines to submit mediocre work.

"Think about the images you've presented and how you might organize them into a more powerful prose," says Leonard.

Effective editing begins with the drafting process, according to columnist and writing coach Jim Stasiowski.

Before writing the first word of your column, know three things:

■ Exactly what you want to say
■ The order in which you want to say it
■ The amount of space you have to say it in

An organized first draft reduces the editing phase. A brief outline may be a helpful guide. Nothing formal, maybe just a few words on a cocktail napkin (if that's when inspiration hits you) that represent the beginning, middle, and end of your piece. Paragraphs should appear in a logical sequence to minimize confusion or skipping around by a reader.

An outline might include:

■ The central conflict of the column (main theme of the story)
■ Subconflicts (contributing factors to the central conflict)
■ Supporting information (relevant facts or data)
■ What is the message of your column?

Rehearsal is a technique Stasiowski uses to gauge readiness to write.

"Simply stand in front of another human being and tell him or her what you're about to write. Do not ask for advice and do not use your notebook as a crib sheet. If you cannot tell your story or argue your column from your brain, you're not ready to write," he says.

With thoughts organized, a draft is prepared. At the screen, you're ready to apply the scalpel. Where to cut? Here are popular suggestions from various columnists:

■ Excise redundancy. Each paragraph should build on, not repeat, a clearly stated premise that appears at the beginning of a column.

■ Go word by word to get rid of the bloat.

■ Reading aloud catches errors not visible to the eye.

■ Keep the "I" of first-person narrative to a minimum because it is distracting. For example, excise "I think, " "I believe," or "Sometimes it occurs to me."

■ Reduce adjectives.

■ Verbs create both movement and mood. Use descriptive verbs in an active tense.

■ Cliché alert. Create original phrasing.

■ Plays on words are overdone.

■ Use easy-to-understand language. "A good, plain, concrete noun and active verb is the best way to write," said Pete Hamill at a 2005 NSNC meeting in Texas.

Blight Begone

Hamill gave a sound beating to the misuse of words, which he described as a "creeping blight" over the language.

"I call it *impactism* and it all comes from whoever the beast was who first used 'impact' as a verb. I think it came out of the government, where the worst language comes from," said Hamill.

He gave some examples of deplorable usage, with corrections in parentheses:

Tasked to do something. ("Task is a noun and should remain a noun," said Hamill).

Transited, as in *he transited to Pakistan.* ("Traveled")

Referenced, as in *"he referenced to..."* ("Referred")

Exited, as in *he exited the taxi and went across the street.* ("When I was growing up in Brooklyn, exit was a noun," said Hamill).

Proactive ("What's the difference between proactive and active? None," he said.)

Perfect Words — But To Whom?

Writers pursue precise words. Some run after them. Wilson finds that jogging loosens up both his muscles and the best words from his brain.

"I go running for words and then that one perfect word shows up and I say, 'There you are. Where have you been?'" he said.

But a "perfect" word may not be perfect to others. There are opposing views on word choices. Does lofty language alienate readers? But then shouldn't writers use excellent expression to fight against "dumbing down" a column?

Consider Hamill's advice to columnists: "You're not supposed to make the audience dumber, but smarter. We must never write down to the reader."

However, columnist and author Greg Rummo of New Jersey recalls the advice from one editor that continues to guide his work.

"I used the word 'tome' instead of thick book, and she cautioned me, 'Don't send readers scrambling for their lexicon.' She also told me that the main reason people read a newspaper is for entertainment. So I keep that in mind," said Rummo who was a top winner of the 2002 Amy Foundation General Journalism Competition.

What to do? Aim for a balance between personal style and a comfortable read for the audience. Trust an editor's suggestions because she is familiar with the newspaper's audience and vernacular.

However, don't rule out sophisticated expression. Words have depth and unfamiliar ones might prod a reader's curiosity for the better. A columnist should model correct usage and grammar, which is part of the education of readers.

Writing "down" to readers is a disservice. Yet, too many high falutin' words strung together can be tiring. (You try holding a five-pound thesaurus as a companion reference). Strike a healthy balance.

When self-editing, is it helpful to get feedback from others?

"Don't read your work to everyone you know — too many people, too many opinions. Find one person whose opinion you trust," advises Beckham.

Cut, excise, rewrite, rephrase. The results will serve up a nourishing tonic to the reader.

"Condensed writing turns the column into a great 'soup' when it's reduced to the most intense flavors," says self-syndicated columnist Maggie Van Ostrand of California.

Far and away the best prize that life offers is the chance to work hard at work worth doing.

Theodore Roosevelt

Elements of a Pulitzer Prize-Winning Column

How is excellent writing examined, considered and deemed worthy of a Pulitzer Prize? Keith Woods, dean of faculty for the Poynter Institute, shares his observations from serving as a two-time Pulitzer jurist and chair of the 2003 column-writing panel. As the Pulitzer jurors culled winners from hundreds of columns, Woods assembled a list of characteristics that defined the best and worst of the entries.

Woods, who teaches writing, reporting, editing, column writing, coverage of race relations, ethics, and diversity at Poynter, talked about those traits in The Winning Column, a workshop he put on at a 2004 NSNC conference in New Orleans. Below is the presentation, revised in 2006.

Elements of Excellence

The best entries shared 10 characteristics. The Winning Column, then:

1. Has a strong voice
2. Informs and enlightens
3. Has a distinct point of view
4. Offers a clear arc
5. Achieves clarity of thought
6. Tells a good tale
7. Is fair, even when critical
8. Demonstrates emotional range

9. Introduces new voices
10. Zigs when others zag

The Down Side
There were also traits that tended to turn off jurists:

1. They're boring, dull or corny
2. The writer is fond of clichés
3. The columnist is a fan of quoting him/herself
4. The voice is too glib, smug or flippant
5. The piece is too "inside baseball"
6. There's no opinion in the column
7. The column is little more than a feature with mug attached

Winning Examples

Excerpts below provide a glimpse of what the winning characteristics look like in action. The writers included below have won most of journalism's top prizes, including several Pulitzer winners.

Winning trait: Stong voice, has a distinct point of voice, achieves clarity of thought

> This is how you stone a woman to death. You bury her up to her neck. Then you heave stones at her head. One imagines her face slowly obliterated, her skull repeatedly broken.
>
> Leonard Pitts, Jr., *The Miami Herald*, Pulitzer winner, 2004

Winning trait: Informs and enlightens

> She has helped 24,000 women overcome obstetric fistulas, a condition almost unknown in the West but indescribably hideous for millions of sufferers in the poorest countries of the world. It typically occurs when a teenage girl cannot deliver a baby because it is too big for her pelvis.
>
> After several days of labor without access to a doctor, the baby dies and the girl is left with a hole between her bladder, vagina and sometimes rectum. The result is that urine and sometimes feces drip constantly down her legs. In some cases, she is also left lame from nerve

damage.

Women with fistulas stink and leave of a trail of urine behind them. They are often abandoned by their husbands and driven out by other villagers.

Perhaps it's because Westerners can't conceive of the horror of obstetric fistulas (American's haven't commonly suffered fistulas since the 19th Century, when a fistula hospital stood on the site of today's Waldorf-Astoria Hotel in Manhattan). Or perhaps the issue doesn't galvanize women's groups because fistulas relate to a traditional child-bearing role.

But talk to the shy, despondent outcasts who are reborn in the Fistula Hospital here and you'll realize there is no higher mission and that Dr. Hamlin is the new Mother Teresa of our age.

Nick Kristoff, *The Washington Post*, Pulitzer winner, 2006

Winning trait: Good tale, clear arc

He boarded the plane and left her a message...He told her he would be home by lunch and would surprise her with a meal he was going to prepare.

Prasanna would wake to his message, and to the televised image of Flight 11 crashing into the tower. That can't be him, she thought. It looks like a small plane, not a jet. That can't be him. They had such plans.

In their regular chats, Kumar reminded Prasanna that therapists were available to help her. But he knew she wouldn't go for it.

"In India, from a cultural point of view, going for that kind of counseling is treated like a stigma, like admitting that something is wrong," says Kumar.

On Friday afternoon, Kumar got an urgent call from USC colleagues. Los Angeles police were at Prasanna's apartment and he was asked to go there immediately.

At the door, an officer asked him if he thought he could handle the task of identifying the body of the young woman inside.

"Yes, of course," he said, holding to a slim hope.

Prasanna had strung the rope over the Nautilus equipment her husband worked out on. Without warning or explanation, she had taken her life, too much grief to carry through a world gone cold.

"I kept wondering if I missed something," says

Kumar, his face full of shadows...

He missed nothing. Prasanna revealed only what she chose to, then followed after her husband, taking a love without limit to a world without end.

Steve Lopez, *Los Angeles Times*, ASNE Commentary winner, 2002

Winning trait: Zigs when others zag

The coroner says he only called it homicide because he had no choice.

Under Ohio law, he explained, his only other options were to categorize the death as accidental, natural or suicide. None of those, he felt, adequately accounted for how Nathaniel Jones died — i.e.,after being beaten with nightsticks wielded by Cincinnati police officers.

The officers say they were only seeking to subdue the 41-year-old black man after he began acting strangely — dancing and barking out numbers — and then became combative during an encounter outside a fast-food restaurant.

Video of the Nov. 30 beating, captured by a camera in a police cruiser, has been played on television nonstop, heightening racial tension in a city where tension doesn't need the help — a city which, two years ago, endured days of street violence after police shot and killed an unarmed black man. Last week's ruling by coroner Carl Parrott appears to have only splashed gasoline on this latest fire.

More Important Factors

This, even though the doctor took pains to stress that the term "homicide" was not meant to suggest "hostile or malign intent." Jones, he pointed out, bore only superficial bruises on his lower body from the beating. Far more important in determining a cause of death were the facts that he weighed 350 pounds, had heart disease and high blood pressure, and was on cocaine and PCP. The coroner ruled that Jones died, in essence, because his heart couldn't take the exertion.

Those caveats aside, Cincinnati police are infuriated by the word "homicide."

Local activists, on the other hand, say it bolsters their contention that Jones was just the latest black man brutalized by police.

I understand their anger. My problem is that I also understand PCP, having lived in Los Angeles during the years that city became the epicenter of its illicit production and use.

PCP is phencyclidine hydrochloride, an animal tranquilizer we knew as angel dust. We also knew that people who were "dusted" might dance naked in the middle of busy intersections or hurl themselves from skyscrapers believing they could fly. PCP users sometimes seemed to possess a freakish strength, an impression created by the fact that the drug leaves some people in a violent, agitated state while simultaneously desensitizing them to pain.

A Dangerous Combination

That would be a dangerous combination in a man who only weighed 120 pounds. Consider it in a man Jones' size and it offers a certain context for the images captured on that video. Might even induce a fair observer to give police the benefit of the doubt.

Of course, where police and black people are concerned, many would say there can be no benefit because there is no doubt: the police are racist, the police are unjust, the police do not value black life as highly as white. End of story.

Except that it's not. For all the many valid reasons black people have to distrust the police, it's a mistake to automatically presume malfeasance on the part of every officer in every encounter. To do that is to put the good cop on the defensive and give the bad cop no incentive to change. Worse, it undercuts African-American moral authority, undermines the argument it purports to advance, makes anger seem not righteous, but reflexive.

The facts as they stand simply do not justify adding this case to the dishonor roll of police misconduct. Jones did not have his head broken like Rodney King. He was not sodomized with a stick like Abner Louima. He was not executed in a doorway like Amadou Diallo. He was, in the final analysis, a morbidly obese man with a diseased heart and high blood pressure who chose to use cocaine, chose to use PCP and then, under their influence, chose to slug it out with cops.

Which is why, from where I sit, there is no choice but

to reach a very different conclusion than the coroner: Nathaniel Jones committed suicide.

Leonard Pitts, Jr., *The Miami Herald*, Pulitzer winner, 2004

The Making of a Columnist

Leonard Pitts, Jr. of The Miami Herald *is syndicated nationally and won a Pulitzer Prize in 2004. In 2002, he was awarded Columnist of the Year by the National Society of Newspaper Columnists for his September 11 column,* We Will Go Forward From Here.

Before the NSNC meeting in 2002 in Pittsburgh, Pitts shared his insights on being a columnist.

I want to talk for a few minutes about how I got here. For the record, I didn't start out to be a columnist when I came out of college, lo those many years ago. Indeed, I had my career all planned, and if you had asked me to write it out for you, you would not have found "columnist" anywhere on the page. No, on the Monday after graduation, I took a job as associate editor of SOUL, which was a nationally-distributed black entertainment newspaper. I was going to work there as a music critic for exactly two years, during which time I would be simultaneously writing the Great American Novel.

I had this book in mind, man ... it would make you laugh, it would make you cry, it would make you gasp. And that was just the table of contents. I'm telling you, this book would be so powerful, so life-changing, that librarians would weep, teachers would write sonnets in my honor and beautiful women would stop me on the street and beg me to father their children.

So you can imagine my surprise when I wake up one day and the Great American Novel is in, like, the 10th draft, and I realize that I've somehow managed to spend 18 years writing about pop music. That's 18 years interviewing Rod Stewart in his hotel suite and loitering around afterward in hopes that Rachel Hunter will walk in any minute. It's nearly two decades asking

Mariah Carey to tell me about her new tour even though the only thing I really want to see her tour is the depths of hell. It's nearly half my life spent trying to find a nice way to tell Barry White — six-foot-something nearly 300 pounds Barry White — that his new album sucks.

Eighteen years. When I started writing about music, Michael Jackson was still black and rap was something you did to a Christmas gift. *Eighteen* years. That's roughly the distance from Barry Manilow to Snoop Dogg. You ever try going from Snoop Dogg to Barry Manilow? From "rollin' down the street smokin' endo sipping on gin and juice" to "I write the songs that make the whole world sing?" You can get whiplash that way.

So inevitably, there came a time when I realized I no longer had the enthusiasm for the job. I can tell you the exact moment, in fact. A U2 concert in late 1993. Sitting in the fourth row at Joe Robbie stadium in Miami — some of the best seats I've ever had for any concert. The lights dim, the band comes on, I stand up with my notepad in hand and my pen poised.

And that's when this human wave comes sweeping down with a mighty roar from the back of the stadium, young people bowling over anything old that happens to be standing in their path. Unfortunately for me, I fit both descriptions. The man who eventually struggled back to his feet was fundamentally differ-ent from the one who had been standing there a moment before. That man gathered his notepad and his wife, left behind some of the best concert seats he'd ever had in his life, and saw the rest of the show from the relative solitude of the nosebleed sec-tion.

I went to my editor not long after that and told him I was about done as a music critic. He asked me what I wanted to do instead. I figured maybe I could be a columnist. He asked me to write a couple of sample pieces. I turned in two of the worst sample columns in the history of journalism. He gave me the job anyway.

I've spent the last eight years trying to learn how to do it. In the process, I have jousted with the Nation of Islam and the Sons of the Confederacy, with the lunatic left and the self-right-eous right, with single mothers and deadbeat dads, with fans of Bill Clinton, George W. Bush and Celine Dion. In the process, I've discovered something about myself. I've learned that I am a bigot. I have nothing against white people, Hispanic people, Arab people, gay people, Jewish people, woman people. But I can't stand stupid people. And, the sad truth is that we live in a world filled with stupid people.

There are, of course, two kinds of stupid. You might call the first kind Homer Simpson stupid. This is the stupid of those who just don't know, the ones who haven't a clue who's buried in Grant's Tomb, couldn't tell you when the War of 1812 was fought if you put a gun to their heads and are honestly surprised to discover that Miss Cleo isn't a Jamaican psychic with the ability to foresee the future.

But there's another kind of stupid. It's the stupid of cold hearts and closed minds. It's mean stupid, ugly stupid, the stupid of the men who killed James Byrd and crucified Matthew Shepard, the stupid of those whose appeal is always to that which is most base, most smug, most self-satisfied. It is a frightening, sickening, eternal kind of stupid.

It's the kind of stupid that makes me happy to have this job.

There was a running joke a few months ago at the Scripps-Howard awards banquet. In accepting her trophy, one reporter gushed that she had the best job in journalism. This naturally ensured that everyone else who trooped to the podium would take a moment to argue that no, in fact, theirs was the best gig in the newsroom. Editors, critics, cartoonists and a bunch of other hacks all going up there to claim that their job was the best.

When it was my turn, I didn't join the debate. Didn't see any need to crush their illusions by saying what was plainly apparent to me. That hands down, case closed, no argument, the people who write columns have the best jobs in the whole newspaper. If you don't agree, I'd like to suggest that maybe you're not doing it right.

As I told an obnoxious reader once in a less-than-charitable moment, "Everybody has an opinion. The difference between us is that I happen to get paid for mine."

Think about that. We get paid to have something everybody has. And on top of that, we are given something everyone else wants. A voice. A megaphone. The ability to be heard.

That's something I value now more than ever. As I'm sure you've heard by now, the whole world changed last September 11th. And the fact that the observation has become a cliché in the nine months since then doesn't make it any less true. Our lives and perceptions are radically different as a result of those fanatics driving three stolen airplanes into iconic office buildings and a fourth into the ground. Everything that comes after is altered, sometimes subtly, sometimes profoundly. We live in the shadow of towers that no longer exist. That includes the dreams we dream, the families we cherish, the movies we watch, the books we read. And it also includes the work we do. Maybe especially the work we do.

You and I get paid to pop off, to spout out, to opine, declaim, criticize, satirize, analyze, fill column inches in the newspaper. Maybe you write about the great social and political issues of the day. Maybe you write family vignettes or Hollywood gossip, gardening tips or advice. Doesn't matter. Since September 11th, we are all working on different aspects of the same story.

It's a story that requires of us the willingness and the ability to take the people who read us beyond knee jerk responses and surface level thinking. Unfortunately a tendency toward knee jerk responses and surface level thinking too often seem to characterize both those of us in the business of peddling opinions and the readers we peddle those opinions too.

It has been said, and I forget by whom, that no one should be allowed to hold an opinion they have not earned. Meaning that whatever your take is on a given topic, you should be able to explain how you got there. What reasoning or logic brought you to that conclusion. You should be able to defend your beliefs against opposing arguments, and if you find that you can't, you should be obliged to reconsider.

To my mind, those are not unreasonable requirements. Yet, it's been my experience that most people can't do those things. Most people believe a thing because they've always believed it. You ask them why and they say, "That's just my opinion. I've got a right to my opinion."

Well, of course you do. But that right, it seems to me, comes complete with a moral obligation to be able defend it. Because let's face it, what you think and believe is not just a matter between you and your conscience. It's a reflection of who and what you are. In the larger sense, a reflection of who and what *we* are as a free society. What we think and believe determines how we vote, which causes we support, how we shape the world.

Which means that the ability to think critically — to weigh and judge and reason and decide — is a fundamental building block of our culture. But so many of us, including many of those in high office, simply do not have that ability. Choose instead to be intellectually lazy and morally unkempt, to be as smug and satisfied in their little universes of indifference and incuriosity as the sages who warned Columbus against sailing off the edge of the Earth.

People ask me sometimes, "Are you a liberal or a conservative." I always say yes. Because when someone asks me to give them a label they can slap on my thinking, it occurs to me that any world view that can be expressed on a bumper sticker probably isn't much of a world view. We look for bumper sticker simplicity, but the world is more complicated than that, demands of us broader minds and larger hearts than that.

Too often, those of us who traffic in opinion for a living don't challenge our readers to understand that. Instead, we hand them the bumper sticker, confirm their biases for and against with numbing predictability and never push them or ourselves to think beyond that. Never ask that they perform the mental acrobatics, the intellectual and emotional heavy lifting necessary to analyze, reconsider, see from another perspective. We set up the straw man and knock him down. Create the caricature and draw a moustache upon it.

Every time I sit down at my desk to write one of my twice-weekly diatribes, I feel compelled to earn the right to my opinion. And a desire to poke and prod my audience until they feel they have to earn theirs, too.

Take the issue of school violence, for example. In recent years, we have seen shootings in Littleton, Colo., West Paducah, Ky., Springfield, Ore., Pearl, Miss., Conyers, Ga., Jonesboro, Ark., Edinboro, Pa., and elsewhere.

How should we respond to that? Should we be comforted by statistics showing that school shootings have actually dropped to historic lows? Should we embrace zero tolerance policies, even though they sometimes mean expelling the child who is caught with a fingernail file in her backpack? Should we clamp down on violent video games and anti-social music or should the crackdown instead be on guns? What do you think? And why do you think it?

How about gay rights? Should same sex couples be allowed to marry or otherwise receive legal recognition of their union? If we say yes, are we endorsing moral decay? If we say no, are we cheating the individual who wants to make medical decisions for a life partner who is seriously ill? Should gay people be allowed to adopt children? To worship in church? To serve openly in the military? What do you think? And why do you think it?

What about race? How do we close this most gaping of American wounds? Is affirmative action fair? Is it a discrimination against whites, a betrayal of bedrock American principles of liberty and justice for all. Or is it a necessary means of redressing the effects of handicaps created by racism — like when you give preferential parking to a person who uses a wheelchair? And if that's the case, are black people really well-served by a society that encourages them to think of themselves as handicapped? What do you think? And why do you think it?

And maybe if we learn to think beyond the obvious on those issues, we can do the same, and encourage our readers to do the same, on terrorism.

Because the questions posed there are new to most of us and more frightening and urgent than any we have faced in a generation. Can we bomb our way back to a feeling of security? Is it realistic to believe we can talk our way there? Was our mistake to choose the wrong friends or to underestimate the wrong enemies? Can we do what we need to do and still remain who we are? Or is who we are a fundamental part of the problem? What do you think? And why do you think it?

Actually, I'm less concerned with what we think than *that* we think. And encourage our readers to do the same.

The world is complexities and it is conundrums, moral compromise and amoral contrivance. And the price of being allowed to use what my editor used to call the vertical personal pronoun, the price of having that little mug shot next to your name, is that you are expected to be able to provide context and perspective, to make it make sense. Or to comfort and amuse them as they struggle to make sense of it on their own.

Best damn job in the newspaper, I still say. But also one of the most demanding. Especially now, in an era of uncertainty and fear that feels not unlike what 1938 must have felt like. In a word: ominous. You can see the clouds massing, lightning flashing behind them. The wind is rising and you can smell the rain and you know, you know, you just *know* tragedy lies ahead. We are going to see a storm before the skies clear again.

You and I don't carry guns, fire hoses or badges, don't make policy or conduct negotiations. But we have a role to play here just the same, if only because it is important for readers to find the people they expect in the places they expect doing the jobs they expect in a time when so much of what we expect has been turned upside down.

They go to your page in the paper, my page in the paper, wanting to know one thing: What do you think and why do you think it?

Give them answers you have earned.

— Leonard Pitts, Jr.

Reprinted with permission

Section 2: Specialty Columns

"You're an internist," I point out kindly, "not a brain surgeon or anything."

"Whereas you're a humor columnist," she shoots back.

"You just proved my point," I say smugly. "Humor columnist is sort of the brain surgery of writing."

W. Bruce Cameron

The Humor Columnist

If laughter brings physical relief, then Erma Bombeck, Art Buchwald, and Dave Barry were a few of the best physicians of our times. Typically, humor columnists don't earn a doctor's salary, but despite the great potential for frugal living, they persist. Many claim faulty DNA wiring and say they have no choice in the matter.

"It's all I've ever done. What else am I qualified to do?" said Art Buchwald.

Often, Dave Barry is asked where he gets his sense of humor — as if the answer might cause a gold rush to the source.

"Who knows where a sense of humor comes from? Nobody knows. I think I get mine from my mom. She reminded me of Erma Bombeck. She was a 1950s housewife but a dark, edgy housewife," said Barry at the 2006 Erma Bombeck Writers' Workshop.

Family humor columns by Erma Bombeck ran in over 700 newspapers before her death in 1996 at the age of 69. Did she ever pinpoint the essence of successful humor?

"She didn't want to discuss it. Sitting down to analyze it didn't do anything to promote it," said her husband Bill Bombeck.

However, back in 1982, Erma Bombeck did offer this advice before the University of Dayton: "In writing humor, the only thing that is important is that you get close enough to the truth to reach people and far enough away not to offend them."

Why Be Funny?

According to a NSNC columnists' survey, salaried newspaper columnists represented a small percentage of humorists. In comparison a greater number of freelancers wrote humor. (Perhaps this suggests that if you insist on laughing over sparely provisioned meals then you're on your own, buddy.)

So what is the carrot in front of these donkeys? Fellow travelers point to love, whether it be giving it or getting it.

For me, I love humor's safe haven. We all hide hurts, build walls and don disguises, (such a poor use of free will), and so laughter is a way to lower our masks.

Bombeck loved the way her readers identified with the desperate hilarity of her homefront.

"Humor writers all have something in common. We share part of our personal and private lives that few other writers share," she said in 1982 before the University of Dayton.

Being loved fueled Buchwald's political satire for over 50 years. On point but devoid of malice, his humor skewered gassy politicians and current events. As an unhappy child living in foster homes, he found his antics equaled positive attention. That discovery led directly to his career.

"I found I could make kids in school laugh and it was the way I could get my love," said Buchwald.

The challenge of the written word is what award winning W. Bruce Cameron loves. His humor columns are syndicated with Creators Syndicate, his *New York Times* bestseller, *8 Simple Rules For Dating My Teenage Daughter*, became a successful TV series, and was followed by his second book, *How to Remodel A Man*.

Cameron says, "I didn't start out writing humor, I wanted to be the next great American novelist. I take the written word very seriously, even when I'm trying to be funny. When I write something down, I care about how the sentence is crafted. There's a rhythm to a joke, and certain words are funny, and certain topics are never funny, so once I begin writing, the craft takes over. I'm driven to make it all come together as artfully as possible."

Write humor because you love it, according to Jerry Zezima of the *Stamford Advocate* (CT) and the *Los Angeles Times-Washington Post News Service*. A humorist for over 20 years, he is a 2006 award winner from the National Society of Newspaper Columnists.

"Your first duty is to write something you think is funny and not to worry about everyone else. Your next duty is to worry about everyone else, which is why humor writing is so hard. Your last duty is to have fun and consider yourself damned lucky to be doing something you love and that, if you are good at it, helps feed your children who selfishly insist on eating," says Zezima.

Being a Jester is a Job

Readers assume humor columnists hee-haw over cocktails, scribble down a few notes, and *voila!* See you tomorrow morning on page 10. More often than not, a call goes out to the muse and emptiness echoes back from the canyon.

Barry won the 1988 Pulitzer Prize for Commentary and his syndicated columns were carried in 500 newspapers.

"I don't believe much in inspiration. It's mechanical," he said before the Erma Bombeck Writers Workshop in 2006.

Every day Barry gets up and writes without fail. He suggested setting a daily word count as a goal. For example, at a 1,000 words per day, at year's end, 365,000 words equal sizable book content. The author of over two dozen books, Barry should know.

Don't count on feeling funny every day because writing humor is a job like anything else. Regardless of divorce or depression your content better be fresh and funny. Don't expect your deadline to be waived just because your dog died. Remember, you're a professional.

Discipline separates the professional humorist from someone with a great sense of humor, according to Lloyd Garver, an on-line humor and sports columnist for www.cbsnews.com and comedy writer for TV shows such as *Sesame Street, Family Ties*, and *Frasier*.

"A professional probably writes every single day, but certainly writes several days a week. Not being funny is not an option. If it takes you until three in the morning, if it means skipping other important things in life, you will make that column funny. The question of whether or not I feel like writing doesn't even come up. It's a job, it's a commitment and you do it," he said.

Finding Funny Fodder

So, how do different columnists create material under deadline?

For me, "fodder-finding" is experiential, like attempting karaoke or joining frenzied Christmas shoppers for the special

5 a.m. discounts. Dialogue carries special inspiration. I can wrap an entire column around one ironic comment overhead at the supermarket.

Zezima finds every day life to be hilarious.

"The best stuff is right under your nose, often in your own home. You don't have to go anywhere, although if you want to put in for mileage anyway, go right ahead."

Cameron's stories are caricatures of real life and creating ideas is constant for the winner of the 2006 Robert Benchley Award for Best Humorist and the 2006 Best Humor Columnist Award from the National Society of Newspaper Columnists.

"It has only gradually occurred to me that not everyone has a brain like mine. I suppose this is a good thing, otherwise we might never have invented the steam engine or the light bulb or Britney Spears. But while other people are concentrating on useful pursuits, my brain is filled with stories, both visual and verbal. It's as if my head is a combination of a multiplex theater and Grand Central Station. I'm either envisioning a movie or hearing whispered fragments of jokes and the only way to get them out of my head is to write them down," says Cameron.

Buchwald was a syndicated columnist with Tribune Media Services, winner of the Pulitzer Prize for Commentary in 1982, and author of 34 books. The National Society of Newspaper Columnists honored him with its Ernie Pyle Lifetime Achievement Award in 2006.

Buchwald earned his daily bread by being quotable, and he summed up his global appeal, "I'm saying something readers want to say and I say it for them."

Dang! He made it look easy:

Tax reform is taking the taxes off things that have been taxed in the past and putting taxes on things that haven't been taxed before.

I always wanted to get into politics, but I was never light enough to make the team.

Every time you think television has hit its lowest ebb, a new program comes along to make you wonder where you thought the ebb was.

People are broad-minded. They'll accept the fact that a person can be an alcoholic, a dope fiend, a wife beater and even a news-paperman, but if a man doesn't drive, there's something wrong with him.

Buchwald's idea process was simple. He read newspaper headlines and was never at a loss for ideas.

"I think the world and our country is much crazier than it used to be. We're all in the insane asylum looking out. There's lots of material," he said.

Humor Treatments

Buchwald's columns averaged about 500 words, and he outlined his writing process with equal brevity.

"Every word counts. There's a beginning to get the audience interested. You have to do it fast. For example, I'm talking about the oil bill being so expensive, that's two to three sentences. Then there's the middle and the end, and the last line has to be really funny."

Buchwald said humor is the most difficult type of writing.

Leaning closer, I asked, "So based on your experience, what is your formula for being funny?"

The longest-running humor columnist on the planet said, "I have no idea."

Formats

Stepping in with a few ideas is award-winning columnist Tim Bete.

Author of *In the Beginning There Were No Diapers*, Bete writes for numerous parenting publications. He is the director of the Erma Bombeck Writers Workshop at the University of Dayton, Ohio, which is comprised of 5,000 humorists. The workshop is held every other year to teach and encourage humor and human-interest writers.

According to Bete, you need a structure, a skeleton, on which to hang the meat of humor writing. Formats provide ready-to-use concepts and also offer the benefits of speed and increased product. His ideas were originally published in *Writers Digest* magazine:

"There are three basic parts to a humor piece: the topic, the format and the individual jokes. Many writers move straight from the topic (say, Valentine's Day gifts) to individual jokes (e.g., I bought my wife a vacuum cleaner for Valentine's Day. She said it sucked) without considering the format. This often results in a list of jokes that work better as a stand-up routine than as a coherent, printed piece. Formats provide a starting point and framework that tie the topic and jokes together," he advised.

Bete outlined five different formats and used Valentine's Day to illustrate the different treatments.

The Diary Format — it provides a chronological structure (e.g., day one, day two) that escalates in exaggeration from the first entry to the last. Example: An escalation of five year's worth of Valentine's Day gifts that gets progressively worse.

The Advice Format — this parodies the "Dear Abby" style, with the questions and answers made up by the writer. Example: "Which gift will tell my wife I love her, a power drill or a table saw?"

The How-Not-To Format — Example: Ten steps to finding the worst Valentine's Day present; or, How I managed to forget Valentine's Day three years in a row.

The Parody Interview Format — Example: An interview with the man who holds the Guinness record for buying the worst Valentine's Day gifts.

The Quiz Format — Example: Will you be in the doghouse? Or, how to tell if your spouse will hate the gift you picked out.

Bete advised humor writers to find new formats by reading non-humorous writing with an eye to how the format can be used for humor.

"The process of running a topic through different formats may provide the concept to write an entire piece. The key is to keep the structure of the piece in mind — you're not looking for individual jokes," he says.

Advice From Dave Barry

Does Dave Barry use humor formats?

This was his e-mail answer, in which he comically created his own Q and A:

I sometimes use the Q&A (Question and Answer) format.
Q: Why?
A: Because you can use up a lot of space without writing a lot of words.
Q: Like this?
A: Exactly.

At a 2007 NSNC meeting in Philadelphia, a few Barry basics on being funny were shared by the master himself:

■ Be funny.

■ Use jokes.

■ Incorporate the word *weasel* whenever possible.

Perhaps not masterful on its face, but the presentation played exactly to Barry's strength. Humor writing only looks effortless.

Being funny in print takes toil and focus. In fact, most humor writers aren't that funny, according to Barry, because they don't make him laugh. He has read countless samples and many are written in a "humorous tone" or are "amusing," but few make it to the summit of Laugh Out Loud.

And to reach that mighty mountaintop, one needs jokes.

Self-amusement is not the same as humor and the hard job of doing humor is putting in the jokes, according to Barry, who said, "It's not an inspired process."

Barry offered a behind-the-scenes look at his own process of creation, and it's comforting to know that coming up with the seemingly spontaneous can involve hours of struggle. Barry doesn't draft an entire humor column at first. He begins with an idea and will spend an hour or two crafting the opening lines, aiming for hilarity.

"Be funny quickly," he said (even though creating that result might take hours to achieve).

Only when he is satisfied with the lead will he move on to the rest of the column, always building on the jokes, and Barry spends time drafting and tweaking each section of his piece.

Mediocre humor lacks the element of surprise, and he urged humorists to avoid being linear. Create the unexpected.

"The unexpected is better than expected humor," he said.

He used the example of air travel. Everyone hates long security lines and the stress of navigating through the airport process. Write about travel and most readers expect a piece along the lines of inconvenience and chaos, so surprise the reader.

"Instead of hating it, try writing about how much you love security," Barry said.

One under-used way of creating humor is actual experience. Go out and find funny situations or create them.

"Do things rather than think things," said Barry.

He once borrowed a giant Weiner Mobile to pick his son up from school. He later drove it to a used car lot and tried to trade it in for smaller model. Truth is stranger than fiction and makes for funny column fodder.

Barry always engages his readers in his writing. Respect their intelligence and their capacity for humor.

"Don't see them as crazy or stupid," he said.

That said, don't be surprised when the humorless take you literally. Barry received waves of hate mail when he suggested Neil Diamond wasn't the world's greatest lyricist, and referred to a rough Diamond: *I am, I said/To no one there/And no one heard at all/Not even the chair.*

But somehow, even through stacks of "you idiot" mail, a good humor columnist makes it through to the end.

And speaking of the end, always remember the punch line should act as both the best and the last part of the piece. Too often, writers don't know when to stop.

"The funniest part is at the end. Don't keep going after that," Barry said.

With moments to spare before leaving for a flight out of Philadelphia, he took a few questions from the audience, and I was the last hand he pointed to. This was my chance for a serious insight into being funny.

"What are your thoughts on humor based on stereotypes?" I asked.

"Leave it to a woman to ask a question like that," Barry said.

And off he flew.

What's So Funny?

The heart of comedy lies in surprise. Zezima summed up two popular ways he zings his readers.

"One is something that comes out of left field — the punchline to a joke, for example. It takes you by surprise.

"The second is the polar opposite: something common. You see yourself in it and you laugh at the familiarity," says Zezima.

Let readers discover the fun as a scene unfolds. Nobody wants to be told what's funny. Laughter Town goes silent if residents read, "A pie hit him in the face and it was hilarious." Oh, really?

The pithy old saying remains true: Show, don't tell.

Plunk the reader down into the middle of the moment when the pie is thrown. Glimpse the joker, hear the whiz, feel the slap of custard. Is that a cinnamon smell in the crust? Eek! It tastes like shaving cream!

If romance novelists "inflame," then humor writers "tickle," and metaphors and similes aid and abet a sense of humor in print.

Here's a quick refresher: a metaphor evokes an image of one thing to describe something entirely different. A simile equates two different images by using the connecting word, "as" or "like."

Unlike standup comedy, a humor column cannot be a machine gun spray of one-liners. Unlike movies, a column doesn't have the advantage of sight gags, facial cues or gestures. Paint with metaphors and similes to color up comedy. Here are some examples:

> Banning books like "The Great Gatsby" or "To Kill a Mockingbird" is like burning down a majestic forest because one of the trees has a four-letter word carved on it and there is a stump shaped like one of the more disreputable bodily organs.
>
> Turn, Don't Burn, The Page by Samantha Bennett,
> *The Pittsburgh Post-Gazette*, 9/28/06

> Place a CD in a stereo and turn up the volume as high as it will go. Repeat this with more stereos in each bedroom of the house. When the decibel level exceeds that of the launch of a space shuttle, open any unbroken windows and see whether your neighbors complain. If they don't, you need either (a) more stereos or (b) different neighbors. You simply cannot fully appreciate the Living-with-Teenagers Experience if your neighbors don't complain about your children.
>
> The Teen-Ready House, by W. Bruce Cameron,
> syndicated columnist, Creators Syndicate

Editors: The Unconvinced Gatekeepers

What's the best way to get your humor column published?

"This is going to sound obvious, but it helps if your writing actually strikes people (that is, people other than yourself) as funny," wrote Barry.

Typically, humor columnists don't enjoy parity with opinion columnists on newspaper pages. Why is that?

One columnist points to a conflict with editors. Samantha Bennett has been with the *Pittsburgh Post Gazette* since 1994, and has written her humor column since 1998. She is a web editor for the features department and won a Matrix Award from Women in Communications in 2000. She serves as the 2006-07 vice president for the National Society of Newspaper Columnists.

"The most aggravating thing is that readers generally enjoy humor columns, while editors generally consider them a waste of increasingly precious space."

Editors typically come from a hard news background, and are inclined to give space to more news-related content, according to Bennett.

"Our editors keep falling back on the 'more local news' mantra. At some point, I am convinced we'll stop trying to sell news content and just host a Webcam service that allows everyone to watch their neighbors at home. Perhaps the government can help us out with that," she says.

If you think getting salaried by a newspaper is the ticket to Humor Columnist Heaven, Bennett will set you straight on the daily reality.

"I tend to hit them in the face with a big shot of cold seltzer. It's a demanding job: Sometimes you just don't feel funny. If you write satire, you will be harangued at length by poor spellers who have completely, breathtakingly, spectacularly missed your point — and hate you. You will be imprisoned in the suburban editions, held for space, rewritten by the humorless, torpedoed with lumpen headlines, left off of the Web site, shunted completely onto the Web site, moved to a different day with no notification to readers, used as filler, and generally treated as if you are using your august journalistic vehicle as a vanity press.

"But the readers who get you...the readers who write to tell you you've made them laugh until they cried...the readers who tell you they've sent your column to friends and relations in other states or countries...they save you. They do your PR for you. They will, some day, buy your book," says Bennett.

Does Barry agree that editors generally find humor to be a waste of space?

"I believe that if editors had a clue what readers wanted to read, they would not be editors," he says.

Finally, The Humorist As Hero

It's common for humor columnists to feel unworthy. I know I did in my fledgling days.

"What kind of column do you write?" someone would ask.

"Oh, humor," I'd say.

In my imagination, they were thinking, "Well, why aren't you writing about stem cell research or gay marriage or the efforts in Nevada to raise the speed limit? You're an ink waster!"

My body language probably gestured back, "Yeah, I know."

But then my perspective changed. Right after the tragedy on September 11, a spirit-crushing sadness pervaded our country, and everyone sought ways to cope. When I wasn't crying, I was numb, finding no comfort in commentary. In looking over my stock of yet-unread books, I came across *Naked* by David Sedaris. His brutal but hilarious memoirs became my lifeline out of sorrow. I laughed because Sedaris gave me no choice.

My hero!

More affirmation came when I read a 2006 interview of Art

Buchwald in *Vanity Fair*. He was asked, "What do you consider your greatest achievement?"

Buchwald said, "Making people laugh. I don't know if it's an achievement, but I love doing it."

Over time, readers would stop me in the street and tell me how they laughed over the latest nonsensical turn in my life. Sometimes I'd mention the possibility of "writing more serious commentary."

"Don't you dare!" was the adamant response.

Today, I suspect many humorists, both striving and accomplished, remain insecure. (Over and above the angst all writers suffer.) I base this on observations made while I was president of the National Society of Newspaper Columnists, when writers would call with a common question:

"Do I stand a chance in contests where humor is included in the general commentary category?"

To me, this translated to, "Real Life v. My Funny Take on Real Life, can I really compete?"

Perhaps the underlying question was, "How important is what I do?"

The benefits of laughter are as tangible as straightening a broken bone or applying a tourniquet. Love, light, and laughter — that's what's in our little black bag. Too bad our type of doctoring doesn't pay for a Jaguar XKR. Therefore, I'm all for revamping our healthcare system.

Oh, life is a glorious cycle of song,
A medley of extemporanea;
And love is thing that can never go wrong;
And I am Marie of Romania.

Dorothy Parker

The Lifestyle Columnist

Intimate writing takes a special kind of columnist. Karin Vingle Fuller of *The Sunday Gazette-Mail* in West Virginia wrote about the death of her baby. Terry Marotta, self-syndicated in Massachusetts, shared with readers the marriage of her gay daughter. Another Bay State columnist, Michael Murphy, poignantly recorded his aging mother's slow deterioration from Alzheimers.

Columns about personal trials and triumphs are a way of asking the reader, "And what about you? Can you imagine being homeless? Did you ever think Paul McCartney would really turn 64? Do you want to search for your birth mother someday?"

"Sometimes we ask readers to go with us to very dark places and think about things they might not want to think about," said Laura Pulfer at a 2006 Erma Bombeck Writers' Workshop. A former columnist for the *Cincinnati Enquirer*, she was inducted into the Cincinnati Journalism Hall of Fame by the Society of Professional Journalists in 1999.

According to Pulfer, a reader needs to believe in a columnist's honesty to go on that journey, and such trust builds over time and with familiarity.

"Socrates said that when you want to persuade people to do something, you must first persuade them you are of good will," said Pulfer.

For the columnist, vulnerability in print takes courage, not only for what is revealed, but also because of negative reaction. The lash stings when readers jeer at, for instance, your divorce or your desire to be a single parent. Expect accusations of navel-gazing or being egocentric or just plain screwy in the head.

Still, the goal of self-revelation is to support, enlighten, inspire or educate the reader, and even a rock bottom experience can serve as a cautionary tale. Personal sharing is double-edged. At its best, a personal column offers readers a warm heart-to-heart or treats them to a shared vicarious thrill. At its worst, a personal column is a narcissistic monologue.

So how does a writer walk the tightrope between self-revelation and being self-absorbed?

Self-revelation works when the reader sees an aspect of his or her life mirrored in the story. Whether it's a class reunion or parachuting at age 60, readers long to understand the world around them a little better by imagining themselves in situations. Maybe a reader would never bungee jump off a bridge, but can identify with the columnist's curiosity, or fear, or bent for adventure. Be mindful of creating a universal subtext within your story; that is, a connection to which readers can relate, for example, creating a sense of belonging. Writing about a subject of wide appeal is an effective way of tapping into common emotions.

It's Not About You

Well, yes, the column is about you, but only as a mirror to the reader. Shared experiences should point attention to larger issues, and give something useful back to the reader. Ask yourself, "How does my experience educate my reader?" or "What do I want my readers to take away from this?"

Self-revelation does its job when a reader thinks, "Wow, that was a good approach," or "How would I have handled that?"

Personal writing is self-absorbed when a reader simply thinks, "Gee, poor thing," or "Well, bully for you."

No Tirades, Please

An emotional reaction from the reader is the payoff for heart-felt writing. But some writers veer more toward venting, offering nothing more than pure unresolved emotion. If outrage sparks the premise of your column, then back it up with well-researched facts and clear reasoning. Channel the drama into something higher — action for the community or attention to important issues.

The Priest is Off Duty

Don't use a column as a public confessional unless readers will learn something from your missteps. A column is not a platform for self-redemption. For instance, giving up a child for adoption is a worthy story to share, and surely readers will feel empathy, but don't force-feed them a list of self-serving reasons. Take them into your dark place, shine the light, but let them return with their own find.

To keep it real, be real. For a decade, six million readers have turned the page to read Craig Wilson's column about life's little moments in the Life Section of *USA Today*. He summed up faux revelation as stiff and unoriginal writing.

"[It's bad] when it's pretentious, or when it's trying to be humorous but it's on the verge of slapstick. There's a subtlety to good writing that surprises. The element of surprise is missing in a lot of bad writing," Wilson said at a 2006 Erma Bombeck Writers' Conference.

Interestingly, writing and hypnosis have much in common. Both arts aim to draw a person in and suspend reality in the hopes of a positive outcome. In 1990, I observed this connection when I took a certification course in hypnotherapy out of a long-time curiosity. Eager to learn how hypnosis worked, I soon discovered that the mechanics of the conscious versus subconscious mind could be applied to writing.

Our conscious mind analyzes the world around us and dictates personal decisions. Our inner critic responds to the question of "why" and listens to words like "should," "ought to," and "must."

Informational columns — for example, metro columns, political commentary, or how-to types of writing — appeal to the conscious mind. They spark debate and analysis and satisfy the fact-finding reader.

On the other hand, our subconscious mind responds to images, feelings, and emotions. This is why childhood stories, myths, and memories are so powerful. When the subconscious is fully engaged, it is possible to bypass the chattering of the conscious mind and enter a focused, relaxed state. Interestingly, such a tranquil state also provides a perfect reading realm.

To better understand the conscious v. subconscious, let's use the subject of managing stress as an example. Your conscious mind will offer advice, facts, and reasons against getting so worked up. (Example: "Really, if you don't knock off all this stress and overeating, you're going to give yourself a heart attack. Didn't you read that recent study?")

But the subconscious mind holds the key to behavioral changes. Down deep, "you gotta wanna," and changes can be activated when the subconscious imagines pictures and can "feel" its way out of stress. (Example: "Imagine yourself before a warm blue sea and take a deep breath and let go. Feel how relaxed you are.")

So how does this apply to writing?

Hypnotherapy training involved the writing of "guided imageries," which were read aloud to induce a meditative state in another. People remained aware of their surroundings, but were very focused and relaxed (just like the perfect reader). These were the guidelines for creating the script:

■ Use words that sound soothing and have a poetic flow.
■ Engage all five senses in an active, experiential way.
■ Paint the relaxation scene with vivid and specific imagery.

For example, if creating a beach scene, are you inches from the water's edge? Sitting on a dune? How does the beach feel? Sandy? Pebbly? What is the temperature? Breezy? Bracing? Do you hear a distant foghorn? Lapping waves? How does the sea smell? Briny? Sweet?

The process for creating hypnotic imagery is similar to a writing workshop. Words can work hypnotically because the subconscious is sensory. Vivid pictures induce a deeper trance by relaxing the listener.

When applying this to column writing, readers are more attentive and involved when they *feel* they are living in the scene. Bring readers right into the experience by writing on an all-sensory level.

I've written poignant vignettes for *The Boston Globe* and this is how I've reached the "heart" of a story. While observing something or recalling a memory, a visceral punch-in-the-gut will spark an idea for a column. For instance, at a "men's cooking class," I observed it was a façade for two elderly widowers to share a meal in a woman's presence. Or there was the time my 11-year old buddy bowed to peer pressure and denied knowing me. She is African-American and I am not.

I freeze-frame that revelatory moment as a physical sensation in my body. At first drafting, I'm not concentrating on the beginning, middle, and end, only the pure emotion of the highlighted instance. What did I see, hear, or feel that opened up a gash of emotion within me? Only when I physically re-sense the experience does the essential story of my column become clear.

By resurrecting my actual feelings I am able to bring my readers into the heart of the story by moving their emotions as well.

Writing indeed is hypnotic when a reader tells a columnist, "Wow, I felt like I was right there."

Telling Somebody Else's Story

Sometimes your narrative might be about somebody else. Such column writing requires actual witness. Go out and bring back observations. Small details give vibrancy to a scene and the big picture will take care of itself when the close-ups reveal the heart of a story. Maybe the glint of a gold Rolex makes a hand wave all the more dismissive. Perhaps the jaunty angle of a bowler on the head of a man in a wheelchair speaks volumes. Breathe life into your vision with unique observations.

"You need the descriptive details from being out in the field, or it's not going to sing. The key is to find the telling details that humanizes them," says columnist Mary McCarty of the *Dayton Daily News.*

At a 2006 Erma Bombeck Writers' Workshop, McCarty and Laura Pulfer suggested ways to mine information during interviews:

Visit a subject at home, if possible.

A person's environment offers a world of clues into his or her character. Plus, people feel more comfortable in their own surroundings and may open up with more information.

Go easy at first

"Start with softball questions. Don't hammer them. They say if you put your lobsters in cold water and raise the heat to simmer, they never know they're cooking," suggested Pulfer.

Put a person at ease by the language you use.

Avoid journalism terms like "interview." Instead, say, "I'd like to talk to you about your story."

Give a little to get a lot. Be conversational.

Explain why you might ask off-the-wall questions.

"I tell them I want to make your story vivid like a movie, so I'll ask you for things like the color of your sweater," explained McCarty.

Sit back and listen

"Don't be afraid of silences. Resist jumping in. Let them feel the impulse to fill that void. Be comfortable with silence and see what happens," she advised.

Readers need to identify with the story

Above all, write in a way that resonates with readers.

"Nobody cares about your mother. Readers are looking for a subtext. Write about her, but in a way that readers would say, 'That's my mother,'" said Pulfer.

Finally, why would some columnists make a career of ... well ... exposing themselves? Columnist and author Terry Marotta is self-syndicated in Massachusetts. For 27 years, she has shared intimate journeys with her readers. Now she hides nothing from us on what she considers the mission behind writing from the heart for readers:

Exposing Yourself

By Terry Marotta

One day at the dawn of my writing career my mate finished reading one of my columns in the Sunday paper and said something that has echoed in my mind ever since.

"I don't see how you can be so open in what you write. I don't even like telling people what I think or feel, never mind putting it in the paper."

It was a remark that has caused me to ask myself countless times since then: Who is really served by writing that is so personal and candid, whether it is about ourselves or others? And why do some of us columnists journey into these more traditionally private realms, especially since to write this way is to leave ourselves open to misunderstanding and even judgment? Do we not risk being labeled narcissists when writing about ourselves? Voyeurs when writing about others? Attention-seeking drama queens in either case?

Yup.

Then why do we do it?

The answer distills down into one point, because of course we do not do it to gain sympathy or understanding or to draw undue attention to ourselves.

We do it because it's our job. We do it because we're columnists. We are not reporters. We are the sensitive antennae, the people charged with getting out and doing our best every day to understand what people are struggling with or mulling over; what makes them laugh, weep, take action.

Reporters talk about what Went Down in any one day, what Got Done — and certainly columnists have to do some of that too. But columnists must also address the Not Yet Done; use all their powers of listening to sense that mystical unseen aquifer that feeds and precedes all action, in the realm of hope and yearning common to us all. And sensing these buried currents is a feat of creative imagination that requires something very specific of the people who would master it. It requires both true candor and a willingness to become truly present to others, with respect and total attention — and I mean wholly present, with no other aim than to simply listen as they struggle to convey what is real for them.

It isn't easy practicing this kind of openness and some would say it's even dangerous. So drilled are we in the importance of "guarding the borders," so to speak, that by the time we're adults most of us have grown a pretty thick protective shell around ourselves. And yet it is this very shell we must crack open if we are to connect on a genuine level with the people we aim to write about.

It takes courage to do this, and the leap of faith, and that most crucial thing of all: the ability to overcome shyness and become self-forgetting.

I started to write the year I concluded my twenties, a decade I had begun with a self-consciousness so acute I couldn't even look at my college professors if I passed them on the campus.

Then three months after Commencement, without so much as a single minute's instruction in the art of pedagogy, I took a job teaching English in a big public high school.

I will never forget standing in that third floor classroom and feeling a single drop of icy sweat slither down my backbone as wave after wave of wised-up teens clattered noisily in to fill the desks. Right in that first week I saw what the job really was: It was stand-up. Improv. A high-wire act without a net — and just plain torture for the self-conscious.

To keep control, I'd position myself between the first rows of their desks. The unintended consequence of this decision was that, inches away from my person, the kids would feel free to speak plainly, critiquing everything about me. They'd mention my shoes, my hair, look down at my hands and examine the state of my nails. It was either die on the spot or say goodbye to all self-consciousness.

So... I did the latter: let self-consciousness drop like a set of longjohns which I stepped out of and kicked away for good, an act I now see as one of the most significant turning points of my life.

And it's a good thing I did, because as I have seen again and again since that time, it is only when we speak from a place of self-forgetting that we can journey forward and begin imagining our way into the experience of others. There was only one way I could help those kids enter imaginatively into the experience of the minds of the fictional characters we were struggling to understand, and that was to try seeing the dreams and fears and urgent yens that were playing upon them as the very same ones that play upon us all.

So, I began by telling stories from my own early life; referring to the times I was lost, the times I cheated, the times when youthful uncertainty had me lying through my teeth about who I was and where I had been. I simply went first, drawing parallels. And darned if they didn't respond with a whole-hearted candor themselves.

It seems that when any one person opens up and says, "This happened to me," his listeners almost instantly reciprocate. "And this happened to me," is how they answer. And when they do this something wonderful happens: clocks cease to run. Fear is banished, anxiety is held at bay. The present moment widens the way the pupil of an eye widens in the presence of something that delights it and true communication begins.

I was lucky to learn this lesson so early in life because it is precisely what allowed me 10 years later to begin producing the kind of personal writing I still do today, in which the same dynamic can be found. So many readers over the years have reached out to me with a candor that matches my own that I now take them for potent guiding escorts in my life, which is what they tell me that I am to them also. It doesn't matter that we have never met, or seen a face or heard a voice we knew to be the other's. We are cherished friends just because we have shared our truths. It is this simple: When you tell a person even a small part of your story, a sense of community is created.

So the columnists who write from the heart help make community. By evoking the inner landscape they also help their readers have a true and authentic visit with themselves.

Over the years in my column I have told about so many things, from the silly to the serious: about my season of criminality when for three whole months I went to my dieters' meetings with five-pound weights alternately stuffed into my clothes or else strategically removed from them, all to cheat the scales and get credit when credit was far from due. About the joys and challenges facing my gay daughter and her partner and the little family they are together fashioning. About the death of my mother at her own birthday celebration: her grey face in the chair, her party clothes torn open by the medical personnel, her little hearing aid parked for weeks afterward on my bureau because I could not throw it out, and the way it started to softly keen one night, on and on in alarm at its own loss of strength, until its battery died and it too fell into the final silence.

When I wrote this last piece in particular people in every stage of mourning wrote me to describe their experience with grief and to thank me for telling them mine. And it was their wise response that helped me at last look at my own history as the child of the father gone by the time I arrived and for the first time to acknowledge emotions I had for 30 years succeeded in keeping myself from feeling.

I learned about the Twelve Steps from them in other words and thanks to them finally came to see that my need to try saving everyone, cheering everyone, easing the sorrows of all humanity was the classic valiant doomed behavior of any child of a drinking or otherwise abandoning parent. And when I wrote about this process I think I heard from every single person in the country who had ever struggled with an addiction or codependency.

We all struggle with our issues; of course we do. What I find so continuously surprising is how often these issues are the same, person to person. All the secret sadness we bear slowly morphs into a kind of querulous grievance that does nothing but hold us back, and make a weight that we need not carry.

It's a truth I was only beginning to understand when my then-11-year-old daughter approached me in the kitchen one day to ask about that absent never-spoken-of figure.

"What about your papa?" Annie said "You never talk

about him. He didn't really just die and leave Grandma a widow, did he?"

I took a long breath and told her everything I knew about that poor man called Hap, who left before I was born and whose face I never once saw — until shortly after my 19th birthday when I went looking for him and found him and passed an hour in his company in the darkened lounge of a hotel in Wilmington, Delaware.

And the moment I was done with my telling she said something that broke the dark spell I hadn't even realized I was under. "I will call my first boy Hap," she said, and in an instant I felt all sense of sorrow and self-pity around my fatherlessness lift from me forever. And when I told this story in my column, I can't tell you how many readers wrote to say, "The little girl is right. Put this to bed. Set down all grievance. Let it go, let it go."

Can it be true that even as strangers we have the power to heal one another? It can and it is, since what the stranger gives us is free, asks no reciprocation, rains down like grace, unearned and unexpected.

I am aware that taken together the stories I have told over the years reveal me in my doubt or blindness, my sad and human mystification. But maybe any column does that. Maybe any column says, in effect, "This is who we were, in the decades surrounding the second millennium. These are the things we hoped for and hungered after."

"It takes a lot of courage to show your dreams to someone else," that joyful truth-telling columnist Erma Bombeck once said, not long before succumbing to complications following a kidney transplant.

Not that we columnists are called upon to be courageous every time, nor are we necessarily courageous very often. But in telling our own truths and in relating the truths of others as they are revealed to us, we bear witness to courage every time we sit down to write.

Shortly before she died, Erma also said that when she stood before God at the end of her life she hoped she wouldn't have a single bit of talent left. "I used everything you gave me," was what she hoped to tell her Creator.

Because don't we all know? It will never be about what we won, or clung to, or kept for ourselves. Always and only it will be about what we let go of and freely passed on, spending our gifts in the service of others.

How better to have used our talents and expressed our thanks for living than to have said how it felt to have been here? We can only say what we felt, or saw, or thought. As columnists we do this every day. How better to have spent a life?

*All truths are easy to understand once they are discovered;
the point is to discover them.*

Galileo Galilei

The Metro Columnist

The metropolitan or "metro" columnist listens to the local heartbeat, and writes about what makes a city tick — and who's doing the ticking off. The metro column is loud with victory yells, government whispers, NIMBY (not-in-my-backyard) ballyhoo, and collective groans. As the community's eyes, the writer examines dark underbellies, public waste, colorful characters, trials, and triumphs on behalf of the readers.

Two metro columnists interviewed here have enjoyed long, award-winning careers.

Tony Messenger is the editorial page editor of *The Springfield News Leader* in Missouri. Previously, he wrote a metro column that appeared four times a week in *The Columbia Daily Tribune*. Over his 15-year career, he has won major writing awards from The National Society of Newspaper Columnists, the Kansas City Press Club, the NAACP, and the Missouri Press Association.

Since 1993 Dave Lieber has worked as a senior columnist for the *Fort Worth Star-Telegram* in Texas. His column, "The Watchdog," holds government and businesses accountable to the community. Over his 30-year career he has received awards from the National Society of Newspaper Columnists, The Press Club of Dallas, and the Dallas/Fort Worth Association of Black Communicators. In the late 1990s, Lieber, an author and speaker, was one of the first to pioneer a "video column."

Messenger and Lieber shared insights into their special calling as metro columnists.

The Metro Columnist

Q: *What makes metro column writing compelling for you?*

TM: We make a difference. We truly change lives. That's the purity of spirit that drives many people into journalism. Whether it's the column that points out public corruption, helps the homeless person find shelter, or gets people thinking about a law that needs to be changed, I know I reach people in a meaningful way. It's powerful and humbling at the same time.

DL: When you think of it, a community has no other real voice. Political leaders have their selfish political interests at heart. Business leaders care about the bottom line. Educators don't have the bully pulpit. Preachers only preach to their denominations. The metro columnist speaks for everyone and gains little in return.

We're the one who dips into the emotional mindset of the readers and helps them to see and, on a good day, to understand, what is happening in their community, good or bad, and why.

Q: *How does one become a metro columnist?*

DL: Luck, patience, and hard work, in that order. Luck because the jobs are rare and impossibly hard to find. Either someone dies or is fired or quits or a newspaper is expanding and creating column jobs. It's more likely your house will be hit by a tornado.

But we live in a nation where achieving your dreams is our creed. I decided I wanted to be a columnist when I was 14. It took me 22 years. I got hired when I was 36. All those years in the meantime, I wrote and wrote and wrote. Everything I did was geared toward learning how to be a columnist. I was a reporter, a magazine writer, anything and everything that would get me closer to my goal.

Q: *What qualities best suit a metro columnist?*

TM: You must be inquisitive, smart, confident, and believe in what you're doing. A columnist above all must believe in journalism and be a good reporter. Struggle for the right words. A columnist must be a good person with a heart and soul who truly cares about making his community a better place.

Q: *How do you investigate and collect so many facts under a deadline?*

TM: The best situation is when a news columnist was previously a reporter in the community. After being a reporter for some time in an area, you can develop the network of sources that allow you to get facts quickly, get tips first, etc.

But the key to being a columnist and collecting facts quickly on deadline is to prioritize. A columnist needs to find that angle that separates his work from that of the reporter working for copy on the front page. In that regard, the information I might need is often more limited than a reporter's.

Sometimes, however, the opposite is true. To really write strongly about a topic, a columnist sometimes has to do much more reporting than a reporter, talking to many people who might never be quoted.

The good news about being a columnist is a relative daily conversation with readers. I love topics that are ongoing news stories because I don't have to tackle the entire topic every day. I can nibble away and continue to get more tips and information as I delve deeper into a topic.

The best advice has been given by the top columnists of our times, such as Mike Royko, Pete Hamill, and Jimmy Breslin.

Get out of the office. Walk the streets. Take the stairs to the second floor of the apartment building. Column writing is about the senses. It's about good reporting that makes the writing come naturally. And you only get that by hitting the streets. That is a constant process. A columnist is always reporting, listening, gathering facts. You just don't know when you're going to use them.

Q: *How do you get people in the spotlight to open up to you about "what's really going on?"*

TM: They have to trust you. It's that simple. Any columnist worth his salt is going to end up crosswise with public officials now and again, hopefully of both major political parties. It's the nature of what we do.

The key is writing with clarity and class so as not to burn bridges. Get it right, and take the same sort of criticism that you dish out. It's about thick skin.

When I take on a public official, I expect to take some heat from them or their supporters, and I take the phone calls personally, stand up to it, and accept and listen to whatever criticism comes my way, and sometimes turn such discussion into further columns. Only in that regard will the big wigs respect you enough to clue you in when they have a big story.

The other trick is to develop such a good group of sources that the big wigs are willing to answer your questions because they figure you already have the answers anyway.

Q: *What's your best method for ferreting out corruption?*

DL: Take the tips that flow through the transom like a waterfall, and use public records and interviews and observations to bring them to life. The tip itself is a starting point, nothing more. You don't even have to know from whom it comes, just the right questions to ask. If the question is a valid one, you can almost always learn the answer, no matter how difficult the journey to the answer is.

Q: *How do you perform quickie investigations?*

DL: I always say that a lazy reporter covering a government or business beat is the main reason that corruption can flourish. An aggressive and sharp reporter will ferret out so much wrongdoing that not only will the situation usually get cleaned up rather quickly, but the next generation of leaders in that institution will constantly look over their shoulders. It does work.

I can do most quickie investigations in a day or two. You become a vacuum cleaner sucking up every piece of information that you can find, both through public records, searches and also interviews. The more you learn, the more you ask. The more you ask, the more you learn. I also count on my newspaper librarian to do a search at the same time I am doing my own search. Between the two of us, we learn an awful lot very, very quickly.

Patterns begin to emerge. Focus the story on one element, not a broad overview of their way of life. I don't determine if someone is a good person, just how they acted in one particular instance that I intend to write about.

Plus, before writing, you always do an on-site visit so you can see what you are writing about.

Finally, tell the subject everything you have learned and everything you intend to write so they have the opportunity to refute your findings before they go into the newspaper, not afterward. This helps eliminate mistakes and, more important, lawsuits.

Q: *In metro writing, what is a common, avoidable mistake?*

TM: We all get in ruts. We all have little easy "trick" columns we hide away for a deadline when a big column falls to the wayside and we are in panic mode. The key is to not fall back on these tricks. Sometimes, when I've turned what I find to be a particularly clever phrase, I'll search our archive to make sure I haven't used it before. I've been guilty of doing that more than once.

Q: *Do you use a "format" to structure your metro column?*

TM: In my opinion, if your writing has too much of a format, it's time to break out of a mold. Part of my voice is that I'm unpredictable.

But I make sure readers stay with the column from beginning to end. Like a good comedian, I like to have something at the end that brings the reader back to the top. Sometimes it's a word or quote, or use of metaphorical language.

But do that too much and it gets predictable.

Q: *What should aspiring metro columnists know?*

DL: It is not important to go to journalism school, but to get a well-rounded liberal arts education in college. Learn about history, art, music, sociology, economics, etc. Otherwise, you come out a one-dimensional figure. You get your journalism training on the college newspaper, not in the classroom.

Read constantly about all types of things, and you should start an extensive filing system about subjects. You really can become an instant expert on subjects if you create files and maintain them well.

Take great care in the cultivation of sources, not friends, but sources. This is the most important part. Develop the ability to get people to trust you and like you instantly. They feel more comfortable. They tell you things they've never told anyone. Develop your sources so they have great confidence in your integrity.

Finally, you don't take no for an answer. No really means that you have to think of another way of asking. Get a friend of the subject's to run interference. Keep talking to the person so they develop trust in you. Never give up. The source admires you and realizes you are the real deal — the one who can bring changes because of your level of expertise, dedication, integrity, and skills.

The rule is perfect: in all matters of opinion our adversaries are insane.

Mark Twain

The Opinion Columnist

Opinion and editorial writing, or "op-ed," is what many readers associate with columnists who write about politics, current events, or trends. Opinion writing has many styles and can include the erudite, the plainspoken, or the provocative.

Maura Casey of *The New York Times* has worked 22 years as an editorial writer, and has won more than 30 state, regional, and nationals awards for journalism, which include the Scripps Howard Foundation's Walker Stone Award for outstanding editorial writing, the Horace Greeley Award, New England's highest award for public service journalism, and the Pulliam Fellowship, given to one editorial writer a year by the Society of Professional Journalists. In 1988, she was editorial page editor of *The Eagle-Tribune* when the staff shared a Pulitzer Prize in reporting.

As a point person on the front lines of interpreting late, breaking news, a columnist is used to taking hits and Casey is no exception. At her previous job at *The Day* in New London, Connecticut, she proudly displayed her favorite pieces of hate mail in her office.

"I had a wall covered with hate mail, like the one that said I should write about things more on my level like 'heroic kindergarten teachers, and misunderstood bimbos,'" she laughs.

Here Casey shares insights into her process for writing an editorial column:

Q: *What is your role as an opinion writer?*

A: My role is to give readers something they can't find anywhere else. If everyone is writing about the problems with Candidate X, and if I choose to write about it, then my job is to find a different angle, a new way to write about it, or a different viewpoint entirely. It's often about picking up a topic, holding it to the light, turning it and seeing a different way to approach it.

Q: *How do you pick your topics?*

A: My first real job in journalism was working for more than four years as an editorial page editor on a page with only one staff member — me — and when you're a one-man band, you have so much to do that you have to become very efficient about finding topics. I wanted to write provocative editorials, but there was no time to navel-gaze. There was certainly not much time to search for topics.

So I trained myself, over the years, that if I reacted strongly to something or if I found myself thinking, "Gee, that's really interesting," then there was probably a topic there.

I'm a fairly ordinary person, so if I react strongly to something, then I suspect the readers might, too, even if it seems trivial.

For example, this September my son is going into the 7th grade, so we started back-to-school shopping. My son's teachers gave me such lengthy lists of required items that I found myself putting it all on a spreadsheet. I had never used a spreadsheet before. I thought that my experience couldn't possibly be unique.

I walked into the office with my cash register receipt, which was 2-1/2 feet long, and one woman said her niece had to buy four composition books and she's only in kindergarten. So I wrote a column about it.

Ideas come from the most ordinary places. You can't follow the pack. If I walk past a person who's talking while waiting for the bus, or I hear somebody say something in a diner, and I find myself thinking, "I never thought of that," then 90 percent of the time it's a column.

Q: *What traits are most helpful to be an editorial writer?*

A: The first is compassion, and the second is curiosity.
The roots of compassion are made of two Latin words, and their original meaning is "to feel with." Unless you can "feel with"

other people, you shouldn't be an op-ed writer. Compassion is more important than being the brightest kid on the block. You have to be able to deal with your subjects. You can't trivialize them.

Q: *What is your process for preparing for, and then writing a column?*

A: My job for *The New York Times* is as an editorial writer. So you read the newspapers. You talk to people — both ordinary and not so ordinary. Once you have an issue you find a way to personalize stories because people always love to hear about other people.

Recently, there's been controversy about women in the military. I want to write about that because my mother was in the Army during World War. II. My jumping off place is that I have my mother's dog tags from 60 years ago (she's been dead nearly 30 years).

Q: *What are your best writing tips?*

A: ■ Clarity of thought
■ Clarity of sentences
■ You must avoid the passive voice. Everything should be active.
■ Simplicity
You don't have to solve all of the world's problems in 700 words. Go with one thought and wrap 700 words around it.

I once heard a wonderful sermon by Father Henri Nouwen who wrote *The Wounded Healer.* He spoke for an hour on one short sentence in the Bible: *It is good that I leave you.*

Taking one thought and keeping it simple is refreshing to readers because you're not trying to stuff ten pounds of potatoes into a one-pound sack. Simplicity is why Shaker furniture is so beautiful. Writing is like that, too.

Q: *For newspaper reporters, it's probably easier to break into op-ed writing because they've developed regular contacts. What advice do you have for freelancers who are trying to develop sources?*

A: You have to start somewhere. Find one person. Interview him. And ask, "Who would you talk to if you were me?"

I went to Las Vegas once for a week to write about the impact of problem gambling on society. I arrived with no more than one or two contacts, and I knew that wouldn't keep me busy for a week. I thought, "How the hell am I going to do this?"

I knew I had to keep my mind open to what's interesting. While driving around Las Vegas, off the Strip, I saw a bookstore called "The Gambler's Book Shop," and it touted itself as the largest bookseller of this one subject.

I entered, and after a few minutes began to talk to the man behind the counter, who turned out to be the owner of the store. I told him I had arrived in town and was supposed to do a series of stories about problem gambling.

He winked at me and said, "I used to be an Associated Press reporter. Sit down and let me look through my Rolodex for you." It was a mile long. Needless to say, I had no problem filling the six days. You can't be afraid to talk to people.

Q: *What sources do you draw from?*

A: You can't beat personal interviews. You can read from a book all day long, but if you talk to a historian you'll always get something better. There's no substitute for talking to somebody. It's a pain, but the art of good writing is surprise, and if you talk to people you will always be surprised and you'll be able to grab onto something for your column.

Q: *What are some things that most people do not realize about editorial writing?*

A: That being able to write opinion is always a privilege. I would be dead in so many other countries to write what I write. The First Amendment is so beautiful. Think about it. It's just forty-five words long, and it contains five rights. Don't demean it by being careless. I see things in print that I wish writers had thought more carefully about.

Life is too short to tear down other people. You can criticize and point stuff out, but you don't have to bring out the brass knuckles, you don't have to name call, you don't have to do that.

Socially, I'm pretty liberal, but some of my dearest friends are socially very conservative. Caring people on all sides of social issues can disagree. That's fine. But I would never want to demean them or portray them as some sort of a caricature. Opinion writers should really think about how they portray people.

If you're not willing to sit down with another person and at least try to understand life as they see it, then find another line of work.

Q: *What do you feel has contributed heavily to your many awards as a writer?*

A: What contributes the most to success is a lot of failure. I love cooking and the only reason I'm a good cook is because I've failed at so many recipes and I've learned what works.

I've learned about good writing by pieces that didn't work. You can't be afraid of failure. Don't think of it as defeat, it's only delayed success. Sometimes those delays take longer than you like, but what has contributed to my ability to write are all my wonderful failures.

Q: *What advice would you give to people who are drawn to do opinion, but are intimidated by this type of writing?*

A: Take the hill. Those were the words of Laird B. Anderson, my professor, who at the time was a lieutenant colonel in the Army Reserves. Military imagery came naturally to him.

One of my theories is the world is slowly, inexorably being swallowed up by bureaucracy. We're all becoming bureaucrats. If you concentrate on all the obstacles, you'll never get anything done.

You have to take the hill. Failure is only delayed success. Learn from the obstacle and keep on going. You can't be afraid to dream big dreams.

Some people would say that sets you up for disappointment, but if you don't dream big dreams, you'll live a life full of regrets.

Four years ago I went on a weekend getaway to Cape Cod with three women friends. We walked on beaches and we talked. One of our friends, a mother with four kids, is so intelligent the air just crackles around her, and she told us she always wanted to go to veterinarian school, but couldn't.

We told her she had to do it. We began to nag her. You can't take a dream and push it into a box or put it away. You'll make yourself physically ill if you do that. Finally, she enrolled in a college just to shut us up and to demonstrate to us how she couldn't do it. Two and one-half years later she graduated with a 3.94 average, and a biology degree. Now she's enrolled in vet school.

You can't give in to your fears, powerful though they may be. We can't have a day without emotions any more than a day without weather, but admit them and then set them aside. That's all part of taking the hill. Sometimes we need other people to help us when we can't take the hill alone.

Q: *How do you handle hate mail?*

A: Don't take it to heart. Remember you've got the last word. If people want to get that upset, at least they're reading you. Sometimes they may even have a point.

My generic response to a critical email is, "You might be right."

My religion consists of a humble admiration of the illimitable superior spirit who reveals himself in the slight details we are able to perceive with our frail and feeble mind.

Albert Einstein

The Religion Columnist

That's funny, me a religion columnist. My new stint as the Faith & Values writer for *The Patriot Ledger* (Mass.) was a surprising twist, considering I had been seeking a slot as a humorist.

To that end, this had been the editor's reply for three years, "We already have a humor columnist, but we love your feature writing, so keep those articles coming." And so I continued to submit freelance pieces on a wide variety of topics. Occasionally, the *Ledger* would run one of my humor pieces as well, and I kept hoping to snag a regular columnist's spot.

One day, the newspaper's gas tank for religion content came up "empty" and the editor called me.

"You've done some of the more interesting stuff. Got any ideas? This page is so hard to do," said Lisa McManus, my then-editor.

Impulsively, I screamed, "Make me your religion columnist, I'll fill up the page! Make me! Make me!"

"OK, I bet you could do it," she said, "I'll send you a schedule."

I hung up, elated. Then it hit me. What did I really know about divinity studies? A former Catholic, I had practiced a pastiche of New Age-Native American-Buddhism for years. Now I'm a Bible-studying Christian. On a newspaper's spiritual compass, where did that put me?

Should I weigh in on Judaism, Christianity, and Islam, with

editorials on Hinduism, Buddhism, and Wicca thrown in for good measure? What was the thin red line between opining and proselytizing? I believe evolution is an intelligent design. While trying to land a humor spot, I had reeled in a religion column — oh, no, what have I done?

Obviously, God has a sense of humor.

With no idea of where to begin, I read the work of other religion columnists. Some used their platforms to preach The Word, unabashedly using Jesus' name and citing scriptures. Others wrote about modern behavior and used the word "character" instead of "morals," but clearly, faith informed their perspectives. Other columnists analyzed religious controversies, wielding arguments like veteran trial lawyers. Some pieces by David Walks-As-Bear, a Native-American columnist in Michigan, imparted a sense of The Great Spirit with folksy simplicity.

Religion writing approaches were wide-ranging and I had yet to formulate my own. Entering a spiritual writing realm called for personal soul-searching. So I asked myself questions, applicable to almost any category of column writing:

Was I in love with having a column, any column, or did religion spark a special passion with me? Religion presented a fascinating challenge, and faith had always been an underpinning in my life. Writing this column offered to deepen my understanding, write about something meaningful, and perhaps inspire encouragement in others. So, yes, I was excited about the prospect.

Then what would be my point of view?

Should I be a faith-based advocate? Or should I be a storyteller of remarkable life journeys? How about a questioning myth-buster? Life is rife with spiritual irony, and I could write comical columns. These are all aspects of my inner spiritual life, so which one should represent my point of view?

What was my personal mission as a religion columnist? What did I want to accomplish with readers? Was laughter the goal? Personal change? Should readers be drawn to explore spirituality? Or should I aim to spark controversy and debate?

How best to use my voice? Readers have described my style as "ironic," "witty," and my personal favorite, "Seinfeldian." Therefore, how would I transfer the writing voice of my humor columns into religion writing, especially if the subjects were serious?

For goodness sakes, where do I go for sources, aside from the General Manager of the Universe?

Oh, this is hard. It was time to call the experts.

"Why do you guys do this?" Aside from my own unplanned

outburst to an editor, what drove others to become religion columnists?

In 2002 and 2003, Tracey O'Shaughnessy of *The Republican American* (Conn.) won Wilbur Awards for her column, *Sunday Reflections*. The Wilbur Award recognizes outstanding work on religious themes in journalism. Why did she add religion editorials to her workload as an editor, reporter, and lifestyle columnist?

"More than 90 percent of Americans say they believe in God and we have the highest church attendance in the Western world. I don't think you can ignore that as a good newsperson. Too often, newspapers are so adamantly secular that they look on all religious people as fanatics. Most of us are just trying to put the goals of empathy and hope into practice. And when something affronts people of faith — whether it's the Madonna painted with cow dung or Muhammad portrayed with a bomb on his turban, it's imperative for columnists in particular to say why it hurts," she says.

Bill Tammeus wrote for the *Kansas City Star* for 36 years, of which 27 were spent as an editorial page columnist. In March 2004 he became a Faith Section columnist, covering faith, ethics, spirituality, and morals. He won several awards from the American Academy of Religion and the National Society of Newspaper Columnists, as well as the David Steele Distinguished Writer Award from the Presbyterian Writers Guild in 2003.

Tammeus described his writing role as "an exegete of the world." (Scholars practice exegesis when they explain or interpret particular texts, especially from the Bible.)

"My job as a columnist is to draw eternal meaning out of what and whom I see around us and to offer the gift of that meaning to my readers," says Tammeus, author of *A Gift Of Meaning* (University of Missouri Press).

Since 9/11, such a role by religion columnists has become increasingly important, according to him.

"They [columnists] help readers understand the many ways in which religion drives the news. They unpack religious motives behind social, cultural, and political movements. They show readers how this or that theological position leads to this or that public policy or action. And they reveal not only the various ways in which religion-run-amok causes disaster but also the ways in which healthy and constructive religion improves the world," Tammeus says.

David Yount syndicated his weekly religion column, *Amazing Grace*, with Scripps Howard News Service in 1994. His national audience was sparked by the critical and commercial success of his first book, *Growing in Faith: A Guide for the Reluctant Christian*. He shared his view of his professional purpose:

"I believe my role as a religion columnist is to comfort the afflicted and afflict the comfortable (notably those who are cocksure of their faith). Some of my readers want me to be more prescriptive. I resist that as preaching. Instead I want readers to think about their responsibilities as men and women who have been blessed by faith," he says.

Yount views himself as "an informer and commentator, not as a preacher," and draws from a spiritual background difficult to pigeonhole by readers. To him, this lends the advantage of unpredictable writing.

"They're bound to gather that I'm a Christian and thoroughly ecumenical, but they'd be hard-pressed to identify my denomination. I'm a Quaker but have three graduate degrees in theology from Roman Catholic universities," says Yount, whose latest book is *Celebrating The Rest of Your Life: A Baby Boomer's Guide to Spirituality* (Augsburg Books, 2005).

A Scary Gig

For myself, my new gig felt scary. Ironically, religion is steeped in teachings of love and kindness, yet the topic can be socially divisive. The public is a label-slapping animal and some factions are ferocious. Though I had not yet decided on my column's direction, already I had conjured up the criticisms.

O'Shaughnessey, a "devout Catholic and committed moderate" offered reassurance. Public responsibility kept her focused on the bottom line.

"I used to shy away from writing about religion because there's always a fear in this country that if you're religious, you must be Elmer Gantry.

"I found that I couldn't really be true to myself as a human being if I wasn't addressing how political/social/cultural events affect me as a woman of faith. As religious matters began to take center stage in the so-called 'culture wars,' I felt a need to speak out as a religious person. To refuse to do so is an abrogation of your responsibility as a journalist and a person of faith," says O'Shaughnessey.

Serving Up Spirituality

So are there helpful do's and don't's to religion writing? Are there pitfalls to be avoided, or a successful format to follow?

One approach is to diversify the appeal of a religion column.

Yount writes about faith and spirituality from a "lifestyle" perspective, and he feels his columns are not confined to the religion section. He seldom writes about church politics and is not limited to writing about Christians and churchgoers. Yount has filed about 600 columns and his work appears on the style pages as well as in op-ed sections.

"What I aim to do is address those issues that a person of faith ought to be thinking about, and feeling some responsibility for. So I find myself writing about everything from cloning to immortality — about love, sex, marriage, childrearing, mortality, illness, suicide, happiness, family life, violence, war and peace, the American Dream, race, ecumenism, prayer, and community. I also write about persons who are admirable or hateful because of what they do or what they preach," says Yount.

He offers guidelines he writes by:

■ A good religion columnist will be an expert on religion in the same way a music critic must rely on a solid education in music.

■ Do not be obviously conservative or liberal. Have broad interests and a clear grounding in faith that lends perspective.

■ Entertain and educate the reader to understand that belief is a great motivator.

■ Avoid sentimentality and easy optimism.

■ Keep a distance from church politics.

■ Admit when you are wrong.

■ Share a sense of humor.

"We were all born naked and never grasp perfectly how to cover up our absurdities. God indeed has a sense of humor; the wise writer seeks to reflect it," advises Yount.

Preparation and ongoing education is vital to be a competent religion columnist. Tammeus, a former president of the National Society of Newspaper Columnists, shares excellent suggestions for building a credible foundation as a religion writer:

■ Acquire a sensitivity to the history and development of many religions.

■ Know what you personally believe and know when to weave that into a column and when not to.

■ Have a long list of sources from many traditions, including academics who study religion but who may not be adherents.

■ Be familiar with useful Web resources — from such spiritual sites as Beliefnet.com to the official sites of various religions and denominations to adherents.com, a generally reliable source of information about numbers. Also know the public information people who represent various faith communities.

■ Be familiar enough with local religious leaders that they will always take your call and trust you to be fair even when they disagree with you.

■ Have the experience of attending worship services outside your own tradition.

■ Know what religious publishers are putting out these days.

■ Read at least one scholarly theological journal. (I'm Presbyterian and therefore I read *Theology Today*, a quarterly published by Princeton Theological Seminary.)

■ Have ready access to a good interfaith calendar and understand which holidays are really important and which are only minor observances.

■ Be readily available to readers by e-mail and telephone and encourage faith communities to put you on their mailing list for newsletters and other alerts. But be clear with readers and sources about how much you can really cover and what is outside your range.

■ Be honest with people you interview about what you know and what you don't know. If you tell a bishop or a lama or a monk or a nun that you need help understanding the nuances of a story, you almost certainly will get the help you need. They want their story told right, and it takes very little to get the tone and details wrong.

■ Read some good world religion books. Huston Smith's work might be the place to start.

■ If possible, travel to countries where the population is made up predominantly of adherents of religions other than the majority religion in America, Christianity.

■ Read good blogs about religion — mine, for instance: bill-tammeus.typepad.com

■ Never imagine it's your job to establish or approve the theology or governance structure or practices of any religious group. But understand how all of that affects the larger public.

■ Know what religious issues are hot in the courts and in other areas of local, state and national government.

■ Understand what it takes in terms of education and other qualifications to become a religious leader, such as a member of the clergy. And get a sense of what disagreements about those qualifications are currently under way in various groups.

■ Get a grasp of how each faith community is governed internally. That will help you avoid giving readers the impression that Pat Robertson, say, speaks for all of Christianity or that Judaism and Islam are monolithic.

■ Ask people in other departments of your newspaper — from sports to the arts to the cop shop — to pass along information and column ideas for you from their arenas.

■ Accept as many public speaking opportunities as you can handle — and use those occasions to encourage readers to contact editors and insist that journalists cover religion more thoroughly than they do now.

Tammeus adds, "Religion is capable of providing a healing presence in the world but it also can create havoc and bloodshed, which is what the 9/11 terrorists did in the name of Islam the day they killed nearly 3,000 people, including my own nephew. And people will never be able to make religion a consistent force for good unless they can understand its breadth and depth more clearly than they do now. Giving readers help to achieve that is the high calling of a faith columnist."

So here I was, listening at the knees of highly accomplished Yodas, trying to envision my own launch as a religion writer and making very unhappy comparisons.

"Oh, gee, I'm not there yet," I sighed.

But sharing spirituality is a gift, and it's wrapped differently for those inclined. I decided my column would tell stories about people who credit their faith for getting them through seemingly impossible events. My point of view would be the "inspired observer." It left room for humor and advanced my column's goal of encouragement.

As my writing matures, (providing the paper doesn't slam its pearly gates on me), I hope depth and insight will shape my column into something worthy of my readership. Improvement will build on experience. That's why I think evolution is an intelligent design.

So along with a sample of David Yount's columns, I share one of my beginning efforts as a budding religion writer.

Righteous woman: Hortense Thomas is 'not preachin', just praisin'

By Suzette Martinez Standring

Hortense Thomas attends worship services of the Boston Church of Christ at Lombardo's in Randolph. She speaks in psalms and has the sturdy, clear-eyed build of someone square with the Lord.

"He will cover you with his feathers and under his wings you will find refuge," said the 59-year-old machinist for Arthur Blank & Co. in Boston.

Her short Afro is flecked with gray, her face is unlined. She recites verses from memory suddenly and often, followed with a smile of certainty.

"It's not preachin', just praisin'," she says.

The world can be hard and ugly. At work, she sometimes locks herself in a bathroom stall and fortifies herself with a scripture or two, because the sarcasm, gossip and foul language can be so discouraging.

Thomas is a righteous woman, unafraid of her truth, but she suspects she comes on too strong. Becoming meek and gentle of heart is something she earnestly works toward. At a church buffet, she sat near the serving table and said, "I'm trying to learn how to control myself because I know I put people off. I'm even reading a book right now. It's called 'Me and My Big Mouth: Your Answer is Right Under Your Nose.'"

A young girl wanders up to the buffet and reaches for another helping of potato salad.

Thomas brings her up short, "Hey! This is the third time I seen you up here! Now don't be taking all the food, leave some for the other people!"

The little girl skulks away.

Thomas again collects her thoughts, "Yeah, 'Me and My Big Mouth' by Joyce Meyer. Have you read it? It's really helpin' me."

Like everybody, she is a work-in-progress.

On Sunday, Thomas gets up on stage to witness. With a ramrod straight posture, her countenance is calm and sure. She was the oldest of 10 children, raised in Tennessee, she said. At age 11, she came home from school to find her mother was gone. Fed up, used up, her mother ran off, tired of the relentless grind of living on a cotton farm.

"I loved my mother so much, it was hard to think she loved me so little, that she'd leave without a word," said Thomas, her voice cracking.

"All hardships are tests. God doesn't make bad things happen. People make bad choices and others get hurt. God's looking to see if we'll seek him out and stick with him through the bad. It was Jesus who said, 'It is not the healthy who need a doctor, but the sick,'" she added.

In the audience, tears fall, ears hear and folks wonder at 10 little children abandoned to each other's care. I listen and think, what a blow to a young girl's sense of self and safety. How do you ever trust again?

Thomas pats her Bible. Overcoming bitterness, getting out of Tennessee, putting herself through school, and later, finding and forgiving her mother are the bona fide miracles of her life.

The way she sees it, her life was being tempered like steel for her later challenges. The Lord knew what she was capable of, long before she did, just like the verse in Jeremiah 1:5 says,

"Before I formed you in the womb, I knew you," quotes Thomas.

During her story, churchgoers at the Boston Church of Christ yell out, "That's right!" or "Help us out!" Amid the applause, some quietly evaluate their own years spent in therapy over a lot less.

"You can't do it without God," she states, raising her hand heavenward, and steps offstage.

A gospel choir raises its voices, 50 singers strong, singing, "I lift my hands in humble praise to you ..." and the chorus lifts the now-standing crowds at Lombardo's even higher.

Thomas steps into the aisles past people clapping. Church members reach out and get back a rock-solid hug of hope. She is the prow of a mighty ship cutting through troubled waters.

Valuing chastity

By David Yount

Recently I was tracked down by a grammar-school classmate I used to date. Although it was nearly 60 years ago, I recalled how uncomfortable her father made me when I picked her up at her home. But after my dating days I became a father myself, and became every bit as protective of my own three daughters.

Shielding daughters comes with parenthood. Male film stars who pursue notoriously promiscuous lives nevertheless protect their own daughters from men like themselves. In effect, womanizing dads preach to their daughters, "Do as I say, not as I do."

Many of us are blessed with short memories, but it wasn't that long ago that Britney Spears in late adolescence took the pledge to remain a virgin until she married. Even at the time it seemed a rash decision for a performer who used sex to sell her songs. But she was raised a conservative Christian and concurred with the value her church placed on virginity.

Every year, hundreds of thousands of American teenagers, boys as well as girls, vow to postpone sex until marriage. Over time, many of them fail but are not proud of the fact. A recent Harvard University study confirmed that virginity vows taken as teens tend to be ineffective, but not pointless — their weakness being that they rely on individual willpower alone.

The popular "True Love Waits" virginity pledge goes like this: "Believing that true love waits, I make a commitment to God, myself, my family, my friends, my future mate and my future children to a lifetime of purity including sexual abstinence from this day until the day I enter a biblical marriage relationship."

The perils inherent in premature sex are clear. For starters, the possibility of pregnancy and sexually transmitted disease. But premature sex also endangers self-esteem, and separating sex from love during adolescence can persist in adulthood, weakening marriage. In recent decades, suicide has become a leading cause of death for teens. Adults handle broken hearts badly enough; adolescents can be devastated by rejection and betrayal.

Author Lauren F. Winner, writing in *The New York Times*, affirms the value of chastity, but notes that it "is not merely about passive waiting (for marriage and children); it is about actively conforming our bodies to the arc of the Gospel and receiving the Holy Spirit right now." Postponing sex accepts that chastity is a gift of God's grace that needs to be prayed for.

And supported by others. Winner believes the churches should learn from the 12-step programs through which people call on God and one another to conquer addictions to alcohol, drugs, gambling and adult promiscuity. Methodist Bishop William Willimon warns that "decisions that are not reinforced and re-formed by the community tend to be short-lived."

St. Augustine fathered a child out of wedlock and was addicted to his mistress. Converted to Christianity, he wavered, famously praying, "Lord, give me chastity, but not yet." If we are serious about the value of virginity for our children, we'll have to agree that keeping it is more than a do-it-yourself project.

(David Yount's latest book is "Celebrating the Rest of Your Life: A Baby Boomer's Guide to Spirituality" [Augsburg]. He answers readers at P.O. Box 2758, Woodbridge, VA 22195 and dyount@erols.com.)

Scripps Howard News Service. Reprinted with permission

I want all my senses engaged. Let me absorb the world's variety and uniqueness.

Maya Angelou

Niche Columns

Write about what you love and do not assume your interest is not interesting. Everywhere, somebody is filling a need with a customized column. Though more narrowly focused, a niche column can stand out in a crowd with higher marketing potential.

Here are some examples of those who write for target audiences:

■ Carol Stocker writes a gardening column for *The Boston Globe*.

■ Style columnist Robin Givhan of *The Washington Post* writes fashion commentary about celebrities and politicians.

■ Brothers Duane and Todd Holze founded The Classified Guys Syndication Company, which sprang from their successful comedy column targeted to the industry of newspaper classified ads.

■ Marybeth Hicks' parenting column, *Then Again*, appears in *The Washington Times* and is self-syndicated to Internet sites. She invites readers to reconsider approaches to childrearing.

■ Patti Lawson penned a column for *The Charlestown Gazette* (WV), *Dogs...Diets...Dating,* and later launched her book, *The Dog Diet: Lighten Up Your Life*.

■ An "items" column has earned Smiley Anders of *The Advocate* (Baton Rouge, LA) multiple awards from the NSNC for his colorful stew of local news, happenings, and gossip.

How do you do it?

Technology columnist Oon Yeoh of *Today* (Singapore) and *The Edge* (Malaysia) shares here how to carve out a specialty niche.

"It goes without saying that you should write about something you know a lot about, but that doesn't mean you have to know everything about your chosen field. Leave that to the real experts.

"You just have to be the journalist who best covers that topic. Remember, a lot of experts don't know how to write well, and certainly not for the masses.

"It helps to be friends with the real experts, so you can tap into their knowledge for your columns.

"Take for example, information technology. That's an area I focus on. I know a fair bit about technology — certainly more than the average Joe — but I don't have a computer science degree.

"I wouldn't be able to write a computer program to save my life, but I do know many people who can churn out software code like I churn out articles. These people are the ones I turn to when I want to understand something complex related to technology.

"My talent is being able to take that information and to convey it in an interesting and easy way for people to understand, and also to give it context. People don't want to just know the facts about something. They want to know how it could change the way they live, work and play.

"As a niche columnist, having depth is not as important as having breadth. The depth can be obtained through knowing the right people and being able to extract relevant information from them. Breadth, however, must be internal. You must have a broad understanding of your field, so that you can cover any topic related to it. So read a lot.

"Lastly, go out on a limb and express strong opinions one way or the other. Take a stance. Readers will admire you for that. They don't want wishy-washy, neither-here-nor-there opinions. They want strong ones," advises Yeoh.

Frank Kaiser's self-syndicated column, *Suddenly Senior*, aims to be a voice for 79 million Americans, age 50+, on issues related to aging. In 1999, in response to his initial queries, national syndicates told him "nobody wanted to read about old people." His first self-syndicated column, "Have Sex The Way You Did 50 Years Ago," proved them wrong.

His work is syndicated in over 76 newspapers, including the

St. Petersburg Times in Florida; and in over a dozen on-line sites. His total circulation of regular newspapers is 2.7 million.

"Most all senior newspapers, of which there are perhaps 500 in the U.S., focus on disease, scams, distress, and death. I wanted *Suddenly Senior* to be the antidote to all that. From the beginning, *Suddenly Senior* had fun with 'senior moments,' 'the downside to longevity,' and (occasional) sex after 60," says Kaiser.

His 3,650-page Web site, www.suddenlysenior.com, features a mix of humor, senior advocacy issues, trivia, travel, and nostalgia. It receives five million hits per month from 131 countries.

Kaiser personally does all the coding for his Web site, which consumes vast amounts of time. However, his Web site brings in significant revenue through advertising and merchandise. How do fees from his newspaper columns compare?

"They pay little. The 300,000+-circulation at the *St. Petersburg Times* is the top-payer by far at $100 a month," he says.

However, like most columnists, the love of writing, not the money, is the big career draw. What is the secret to his so-far successful, seven-year run as a premier resource for older adults?

"I try my best to be provocative, humorous, brutally honest, to say what others dare not say, to push buttons, to break through denial, to be as big a pain-in-the-ass as I possibly can be to a government in collusion with drug and insurance companies out to fleece my fellow seniors and Americans," says Kaiser.

What is your personal passion? Write about it. I once had a teacher who exhorted us to celebrate our own unique beauty, no matter what we looked like. He said, "Even if you have a crooked nose with a lump on the end of it, somebody out there will dig it."

Perhaps the same holds true about niche column writing.

Section 3:
A Columnist's Inner World

Be who you are and say what you feel, because those who mind don't matter and those who matter don't mind.

Dr. Seuss

Who Are These People?

Writing a column "x" times a week is like...? Sex, said columnists in a 2006 demographic survey. So does that make the process luscious or laughable? Maybe both. Then again, maybe it suggests that if left to a professional, the job is done neatly under deadline, leaving readers with a little glow in their day.

Actually, "Sex" was the runner-up in the survey; the top choice was "Pain/Burden/Job." Still other descriptions likened column writing to a dream job, a letter or talk with a friend, therapy, or exposing oneself publicly. What goes on in the mind of a columnist?

The survey mentioned above was conducted by the National Society of Newspaper Columnists under my presidency in collaboration with the University of San Francisco's Media Studies department under the direction of J. Michael Robertson, Ph.D. Initial findings were released in 2006 at the annual NSNC meeting in Boston.

From about 500 NSNC members, 154 responded. USF plans to continue polling columnists by approaching other journalism organizations. Therefore it states the survey results below cannot be deemed wholly representative or conclusive yet.

However, first findings seem telling. Here are some highlights:

Personal

About 96 percent of the respondents were Caucasian. The

majority age of responding columnists was "40+ years old," and the median age for both salaried and freelancers was 51. (Big oops: the survey failed to ask about gender.)

Regarding highest level of education attained, about 48 percent of freelancers and 53 percent of those salaried by newspapers held B.A. degrees. Additionally, 23 percent of freelancers and 28 percent of those salaried had attained master's degrees.

Circulation

How many papers carry your column?

Among freelancers, 52 percent were carried in one newspaper and 28 percent were published in 2-5 publications.

In comparison, 72 percent of salaried columnists wrote for one paper, while 15 percent of their colleagues ran in 20 or more newspapers (the 15 percent likely referred to those working for major syndicates as well).

Longevity

How long have you been a columnist?

The median for longevity for all surveyed columnists was seven years, with a reported career range of 45 years to two months.

The percentage of columnists working five years or less was 34 percent for those salaried by newspapers compared to 48 percent for freelancers.

Other duties

Question to salaried newspaper columnists: If you are a part-time newspaper columnist, what are your other duties?

Editor: 22 percent
Many tasks: 22 percent
Reporter: 14 percent
Editorial writer: 8 percent
Copy/Design: 6 percent

Guidelines

Were you given clear ground rules for your column?

Freelancers: 25 percent Yes; 75 percent No
Salaried: 17 percent Yes; 83 percent No

What were the most important of these grounds rules?

Comments from various freelancers: "Stay local," "no politics," "little first person," "be upbeat," "be funny," "check spelling," "no anonymous sources," "strong analysis, not just opinion," "still wondering."

Comments from salaried newspaper columnists:
"Local news," "no rules, just write," "don't start a union," "report," "don't just sit in a room by yourself," "get content approval," "convey to a reader 'my personality,'" "don't refer to primates in every column," "I'm a veteran, it was understood."

Note: One columnist made his/her own personal ground rule: "Not a word gets changed without my input."

Money

How much do you make?

$50,000 to $60,000 was the median for salaried newspaper columnists, with a reported range of $20,000 to $154,000.

Among freelancers, $50 was the median charge for a column, with a range of $5 to $300. Freelancers reported a median of 10 percent as the percentage of income earned by column writing.

Do you receive compensation if your columns run on-line?

A resounding "No" from 93 percent of everyone polled.

Over the past ten years, my salary as a columnist has done what in terms of inflation?

Trailed: Freelance — 74 percent, Salaried — 48 percent
Kept pace: 24 percent, 42 percent
Exceeded: 2 percent, 10 percent

Regarding speeches, 33 out of 59 salaried columnists said they gave about 5-10 public talks per year, with a median of 71 percent of appearances "almost always free." Compensation for those who got it ranged from $25 to $1,500.

In comparison, 40 of 81 freelancers gave 3-6 speeches annually, with a median of 37 percent of appearances "almost always free," with a median compensation at $250.

More salaried columnists than freelancers reported that they feel "more secure in my job."

Process and Production

"Qualities that contribute to success in column writing" were rated in order, from highest to lowest values:

■ Create narratives/stories in ways regular reporters cannot.

■ Write in a colorful individual style (syntax, word choice,

lively metaphors.)
- Provide an interpretation of events that reporters do not provide.
- Inform the community about important issues or facts.
- Represent the values of the average newspaper reader.

How long does it take to write a column?
Overall median: 2 to 4 hours.
Salaried columnists said writing a column took anywhere from one hour to two days. Freelancers reported ten minutes to several months.

How often do you write?
Among freelancers, 53 percent wrote weekly columns, while 28 percent of their colleagues wrote bimonthly or monthly.
Among those salaried, 86 percent of "full-time" columnists wrote 2 times a week or more, while 66 percent of salaried "part-time columnists" wrote weekly.

How often have you had a column killed? (All responses)
Never: 52 percent
1-5 times: 46 percent

I am working on more than three or more columns at a time.
(All responses)
Yes: 41 percent
No: 59 percent

How many columns have you had published?
The median among freelancers was 400-500, with a given range of 24 to 3,000 published columns.
In comparison, the median among salaried columnists was 1,000-1,500, with a given range of 25 to 7,500.

Subject Matter

What topics draw the most reader response?
Freelancers: Personal Life — 43 percent; Politics/Controversy — 21 percent
Salaried: Politics/Controversy — 50 percent; Personal Life — 21 percent
Freelancers more often believed "serial autobiography" was the primary attraction for their readers, i.e., how the columnist lives and thinks, daily life, triumphs and tribulations.

What type of columns do you write?

Among freelancers: Humor — 51 percen; Commentary — 19 percent; General Interest — 7 percent; Politics — 6 percent; and Metro — 2 percent.

Among salaried: Humor — 37 percent; Commentary — 22 percent; Metro — 19 percent; Politics — 14 percent; and General Interest — 7 percent.

New Trends

Do you have a personal blog that is not part of your job?
Freelancers: 77 percent No.
Salaried: 88 percent No.

Has the growing number of blogs changed your column writing?
Freelancers: 90 percent No.
Salaried: 82 percent No.

What are the most promising niches for new columnists?
On-Line: Freelancers — 10 percent, Salaried — 6 percent
Politics: 8 percent, 3 percent
Humor: 8 percent, 3 percent
Niche*: 3 percent, 25 percent
* "Niche" indicates an overall term for specialty columns, such as technology, science, etc.

Who has replaced a staff columnist who left your newspaper?
A new staff columnist: 40 percent
Freelance or wire service: 27 percent
Nothing: 33 percent

Motivation and mindset

The leading "sources of satisfaction to a columnist" were rated from highest to lowest values:
■ Freedom of aesthetic/creative expression
■ Freedom to present one's own opinions
■ Helping others
■ Fame
■ Money

How do the following factors affect your writing?
Columnists rated influences from highest to lowest:
■ Frequency
■ Audience
■ Length

■ Editors
■ Deadlines

The majority of columnists polled did not believe "columnists should be objective." However, the same majority felt "a columnist should be fair."

Overall, columnists "agreed" with the following statements:
■ "Good columnists are also good reporters."
■ "Column writing is an art rather than a craft." (Humor columnists particularly endorsed this idea.)

Most salaried columnists agreed with the following:
■ "My co-workers think being a columnist is easier than being a news reporter, features writer, or editor." (Most freelancers offered no opinion or agreed).
■ "I am consulted by my editors before they make changes to my column." (In comparison, a low percentage of freelancers were consulted on edits.)
■ "Columnists should be paid more than the average newspaper reporter or editor." (Freelancers largely offered no opinion.)
■ Death threats — more salaried columnists (51 percent) received 1-5 threats than did freelancers (13 percent).

Entertainment v. public discussion suggested an interesting mindset among columnists:

Columnists expressed strong disagreement with the following statement: "It is acceptable for columnists to espouse unpopular or controversial positions not because they believe in such positions but to make their work entertaining." (29 percent Agree; 66 percent Disagree)

However, columnists were somewhat divided over the statement, "It is acceptable for columnists to espouse unpopular or controversial positions not because they believe in such positions but to promote public discussion of such issues." (49 percent Agree; 45 percent Disagree)

Is it worth it?

The survey ended with this question: "And if you knew then what you know now, would you still be a columnist?"

Yes — 95 percent

A good name is better than the finest perfume....

Ecclesiastes 7:1

Ethics

Yours is a coveted platform. A column can spark debate, offer instruction, entertain, or muster support for worthy causes. Popularity (or notoriety) may bring publishing or speaking opportunities. Writing a column can open doors for the writer.

However, to some the columnist *is* the "door opener" and agenda-pushers will court writers in a variety of ways. The dark side emerges when conflicts of interest and appearances of impropriety threaten a writer's credibility. Some columnists have destroyed their careers by cutting corners with plagiarism or fabricating people or events.

Other actions run afoul of ethical practices, such as using one's column as a vendetta or advancing a paid-for opinion. Accepting gifts can be questionable. The subject of ethics is wide-ranging, but it boils down to being fair, trustworthy, and accurate.

Real People, Please

One misperception is that since column writing involves storytelling, stretching the facts for the sake of a good tale is okay. Wrong — generally, speaking.

Unless your column is defined by satire or a parable-type of writing, then readers expect your details to be factual. Other than such exceptions, a column cannot be created by using fictitious people, places, or made up events. Exaggerations and embellishments are forms of lying. Resist the temptation to doctor up dialogue to make your subject "sound better." A columnist who observes and reports on real life is not paid to be a short story fiction writer, unless the reader is alerted to the exception.

Some columnists are well known for using fictitious characters and events to make their point, such as humorist Art Buchwald. In those cases, the audience is aware of such a columnist's satirical style.

However, sometimes a columnist known for factual writing suddenly turns to spoof for a change of pace. Be aware that this can cause confusion to some readers, so make sure they are in on the joke.

"In the use of humor or satire, the reader should clearly understand the writing is in fun. Do not underestimate the reader's willingness to take things literally. Every column must include assurances or winks so readers will know if your stuff is first-person journalism, spinning punditry, or honest nonsense," advises Ben Pollock, an editor with *The Arkansas Democrat-Gazette*.

Be There

A first-person narrative requires firsthand witness of an event. If you write, "The mob became a swinging fist..." then readers assume you witnessed the scene — not your friend or colleague who has a photographic memory and uncanny ear for dialogue.

Likewise, do not submit a story written in advance of an event as if it had already happened. Bad things happen if you try to profit as a prophet.

Who Sez?

Accurate attribution is vital. It means letting the reader know the source of facts, statistics, or studies. Especially important is naming the source when someone is quoted. Newspapers can differ in their attribution policies. The Poynter Institute is a respected education source for the journalism field. On its website, www.poynter.org, *Attribution: Discussion and Debate* summarized perspectives from the strictest to most relaxed:

Most strict: Anything the reporter does not know first-hand by way of eye-witness experience or established knowledge must be attributed to a named source.

Middle: Unnamed sources may be used, only as a last resort, if the information is of special public importance, if there is no other way to reveal it, if the source is reliable, and if the source's biases are revealed.

Most relaxed: Excessive attribution clutters reports and narratives, especially when events not witnessed are reconstructed by reporting. It's the reporter's job to verify the story, to reveal all sources to the editor, and to attribute on a need-to-know basis for the reader.

Walter Brasch, a syndicated columnist and former news reporter, has won over 100 regional and national awards from journalism organizations. A university journalism professor, he shared thoughts on other aspects of attribution:

Citing anonymous sources or changing a source's name

Examples of "veiled sources" can appear as, "Today a source close to the president said..." or "anonymous sources report..."

Veiling someone's identity might be necessary if revelation threatens a person's life or job, but camouflage should be the exception rather than the rule, according to Brasch.

"If you must change the name, it should be noted why. I personally hate the veiled news source. It casts doubt upon the credibility of the columnist, and it's also too easy to say to a source, 'I'll protect you and disguise your name.'

"Make a source sweat. Often you should be questioning the credibility of the news source and asking why does this person want to give me this information? What's in it for them? Are they using me to advance their own political or personal agenda?" he says.

Disclosing a shared source or relationship

Columnists sometimes use an information source employed by a sister organization. For example, *The Washington Post* and *Newsweek* are owned by the same company, and reporters for both publications share sources with each other. The connection may not be apparent to readers and should be disclosed, according to Brasch.

Likewise, a personal or professional relationship between the columnist and the subject should be disclosed to readers.

"Always state your connection. Sometimes it's a tag at the end of a column," he says.

Change what I said, please

You've done an interview and scored some great quotes and details for your column. Then the interviewee gets a case of speaker's remorse and calls back, asking to change his or her statements. Are you obligated to go with the new, "improved" quotes, which may change or even possibly sink your story?

"We all have verbal diarrhea at some point," says Brasch, who suggests tape recording interviews. Generally, for a "hard news" interview, the original statements will stand. When interviewees request (or demand) changes, Brasch will try to discover the underlying influence:

- Did he/she become scared?
- Is he/she manipulating me or someone else?
- Did he/she lie to me the first time and is now recanting?

"I'd try to find out what the truth is, and *that* may be a good insight into the personality," says Brasch.

It's an individual call, according to many columnists.

Bill Tammeus of *The Kansas City Star* says, "I'd be wary of anyone who wanted to do a 180° on quotes. Sounds like someone who is pretty unstable and perhaps not worth using in a column."

He will ask the interviewee to submit requested changes in writing, but Tammeus will retain the right to make the final decision.

Dave Lieber of the *Fort Worth Star-Telegram* might be sympathetic to the inexperienced subject. He sometimes consults with his editor when changes are requested.

"If it's a little grandmother who is not familiar with the rules of the press, she usually gets to make this decision and we respect it. If it is a public figure, it is usually always NO," says Lieber.

Lindor Reynolds of *The Winnipeg Free Press* typically tapes her interviews.

"If they're calling for the purpose of clarity (i.e., 'When I said this, I hope you understood I meant, etc.'), I might give them some leeway. That said, if I have identified myself as a journalist, told someone they are being taped, and then proceeded to ask my questions, it's on the record."

Maura Casey of *The New York Times* says, "I'd refer them to psychiatric help and throw out my notes, because the interview is useless if I can't depend on the information. So I wouldn't use the material at all."

Being Beholden

Gifts, tickets, or trips may influence a columnist to be favorably disposed to a subject. Interviewing celebrities or high-ranking politicians is heady stuff. The desire to be liked or to protect one's access to privileges and perks can compromise independent writing.

"The most important person is the reader, not the source, not the editor. The columnist needs to keep in mind what the reader wants and needs," says Brasch.

And what the reader wants is a fiercely independent opinion. The exposé or unflattering profile is difficult to write when it involves your tennis buddy. Increasingly, columnists and journalists socialize with their sources, all in the name of "getting information." As a result, columnists become part of the culture they report on and submit stories editors might run as entertaining, but that are not newsworthy to readers, according to Brasch.

"Journalists go to parties, they want nice seats on Air Force One. They are no longer keeping a distance and observing and reporting," he says.

Accepting Gifts

Some columnists receive gifts. They might be promotional items to get attention, such as pens or knickknacks. Sometimes they are offered valuable things, such as free restaurant dinners or sports passes. Many newspapers have policies regarding what can or cannot be accepted.

However, is it ethical to accept a gift? Where is the line drawn? Should a keychain and a free day on a golf course be treated equally?

Tracey O'Shaughnessy is a columnist, reporter, and editor for *The Republican American* (Waterbury, Conn.) If writing a review, she will accept books, press tickets to performances, or art catalogues for exhibits because it is part of the information needed to write her piece.

Otherwise she declines gifts and informs their givers the items will be donated to a local shelter she supports.

"They can use mugs, t-shirts, and chocolates far more than I can," she says.

Columnist Smiley Anders of *The Advocate* (Baton Rouge, La.) loves his stash of gift coffee mugs. If a local vendor brings in a box of spicy potato chips, he'll happily munch them.

"I think you can go overboard on the not-accepting thing. The *Advocate* says 'token-value' gifts are acceptable, but anything that could be considered 'a bribe for special coverage' must be returned," says Anders.

Reynolds says, "My credibility is my currency. I can't be beholden to anyone in this city. You need to determine a moral line and stick to it."

She doesn't sweat the small stuff, but, for example, will not allow a politician to buy her a meal. She feels it is inappropriate and sends the wrong message. Yet, there are times when accepting a token is the gracious thing to do.

"If I am reading to a kindergarten class during Raise-A-Reader month and they hand me a school coffee mug filled with jelly beans, I accept it. The teacher is trying to teach them grace and how to show appreciation. It would be churlish to refuse," says Reynolds.

Brasch is author of 16 books, most of which fuse historical and contemporary social issues. Among the books are: *America's Unpatriotic Acts: The Federal Government's Violation of Constitutional and Civil Rights* (2005), *Sex and the Single Beer Can: Probing The Media and American Culture* (2006), and *'Unacceptable': The Federal Response to Hurricane Katrina* (2006).

He believes all gifts affect the receiver, if only subconsciously, and he suggested these questions as a simple self-test:

■ Does this gift compromise your perception? Does it make you feel even a bit friendlier toward the source?

■ How might receiving such a gift look to the readers if they knew? Would your credibility be questioned?

■ Without "samples" or free admission, is the event something you would have covered anyway?

■ Can you make the distinction between something sent for evaluation purposes vs. an enticement toward advertising or a favorable column?

Post-story "thank you" gifts can pose the same temptation as gifts sent in advance. They might set up a columnist's hopes for future "rewards." The giver might have expectations as well.

"A thank you gift is good PR — but bad journalism. The possible expectation is that there might be other stories in the future, that the journalist might somehow subconsciously remember the gift and be a bit more friendly to the source," says Brasch.

Accepting Fees

Accepting money from a person or a group may appear compromising to the columnist. The obvious sin is outright payola for an endorsed opinion. But what about speaking fees when columnists are invited to give keynotes to community groups or organizations?

Some newspapers avoid any perception of special endorsements, and will not allow columnists in their employ to accept a speaking fee. Others leave it to the columnist's judgment.

Freelance columnists typically have more flexibility.

Tammeus believes a general rule is that journalists and columnists should not accept honoraria from groups they write about. An editor should approve acceptance of a fee by an employed columnist. But not all speaking engagements pose a conflict of interest.

"There may be cases in which accepting such pay poses no ethical problems. For instance, if I have a Down Syndrome son and I'm active in a national Down Syndrome group — but I write local politics in my column — I see no reason not to allow me to accept a speaking fee to go to, say, Philadelphia, to address the national group's annual conference so I can speak about our family's experience," he says.

Typically, Tammeus voluntarily donates proceeds to charity.

Reynolds says, "I don't accept speaking fees. I tell event organizers I would like them to make a donation to our local food bank instead."

Anders says, "I don't charge for speaking, but if an organization routinely pays speakers I will accept payment if it's offered. I just don't ask for it."

Yet there are many columnists whose careers involve paid public speaking. In addition to column writing, maybe they are book authors, media personalities, or performers. Their public appearances might include keynote or motivational speeches, emcee duties, workshops, or radio hosting. Some newspaper-employed columnists, such as Dave Lieber, pursue a paid speaking career.

Lieber self-published a book, *The Dog of My Nightmares,* and often is a featured speaker before groups and associations — all in addition and independently of his salaried newspaper duties at the *Fort Worth Star Telegram.*

These are his personal guidelines:

■ No acceptance of fees from any groups or associations within his newspaper's circulation area.

■ If offered an honorarium within his paper's circulation area, he will do one of three things:
- Turn it down.
- Donate the fee to one of his favorite charities.
- Offer the group his books and CDs in an amount equal to the speaking fee, which can be used as future gifts.

■ For out-of-town speaking dates, Lieber will apply these guidelines:
- He abides by the rules set down by his newspaper.
- He informs management of the details of the engagement.
- He will never write anything about the group "for the rest

of eternity to avoid a conflict of interest."

Therefore, Lieber is choosy about which groups he will address. For example, he solicited the North American Menopause Society.

"If accepted as a speaker, it is highly unlikely that I would be writing about menopausal issues anyway," he says.

Different situations and opportunities come up regularly. A columnist strives to avoid conflicts of interest and improper dealings, and will make an individual judgment call based on the circumstances.

Be guided by this question: If the readers knew the entire story behind my accepting this gift (ticket, meal, trip, fee), what would they think?

Long Island Lolita Meets the Journalistic Lowlife

By Walter Brasch

Chapter excerpt from Sex and the Single Beer Can: Probing The Media and American Culture *(2006) by Walter Brasch (Reprint permission granted).*

It was 6 a.m., Monday, when the phone rang, so I knew it was Marshbaum eager to involve me in his latest scam. I wasn't disappointed.

"Got any extra money?" he whispered.

"Not since I became a humor columnist," I replied.

"Too bad," said Marshbaum. "I'll take it elsewhere."

"Take what elsewhere?" I asked sleepily.

"Revelations about my life with Amy Fisher."

"You had a life with the Long Island Lolita? The teen who shot the wife of her lover?"

"Actually, I once bought some fabric at the sewing store her parents own, but I figure what they told me about their daughter is worth a few thousand on the journalistic market."

"What'd they tell you?" I asked.

"Not so fast. It'll cost you. You been looking at the tabloids lately? They pay real good for my kind of news."

"Look, Marshbaum," I said, "The papers I write my column for are ethical. Usually. They won't pay for revelations."

"Everyone else is!" he snapped. "Three hundred thousand to the woman who got shot and her husband who either was or wasn't Amy's pizza-eating pimp. Fifty thou to some boyfriend. A bundle to a trigger-man. Quarter million to some hack to write a paperback about all this. Thousands to just about anyone who ever lived in the same country she did. Millions to produce the Amy Fisher Film Festival on TV. Add in a half-dozen tabloid TV shows, a few talk shows, and all the local news, and you have a billion dollar Amy Industry."

"But, that's schlock entertainment," I said. "Newspapers are more into news."

"Yeah," he said sarcastically, "like the New York papers that have photographers staking out everyone's houses? Or, the battalion of reporters who invaded her upper class hometown to talk to all the neighbors? What about the newspaper reporters who are being paid by the entertainment industry to be 'consultants'?"

"I have no desire to write about sex-crazed teenagers on the prowl for body-shop repairmen," I said. "Besides, every hour they take to report on this teenage prostitute with a Fatal Attraction complex is one hour less they can investigate corruption. Every inch they use in every paper is one inch less than can be devoted to stories about the economy and health care crises."

"What about a scoop on body-shop repairmen who lure teenage girls into lives of crime?" he asked. "I can sell that one a little cheaper."

"He may have been a sleaze," I said, "but there's no evidence he asked his alleged lover to kill his wife."

"Precisely," said Marshbaum. "There's no evidence of any of this, but already TV has devoted more air time to it than they did the Gulf War and the Presidential campaign. Besides, you're the only one who hasn't written about it. Aren't your editors concerned that you're not giving them the latest news? Sin sells papers. Makes money for publishers. Publishers reward sinners by increasing their salaries. Frankly, you're well behind at the moment."

"OK, Marshbaum, what choice piece of trivia did you learn that'll save my career and get me the Pulitzer Prize for Sen-sational Journalism?"

"Like I said, I'm no fool. This stuff's too hot to entrust to someone not willing to pay."

"I said I had ethics."

"Ethics don't pay the bill at Victoria's Secret," he said. "Besides, it's relatively simple. You get the scoop on why Amy's parents never thought it was unusual that their 16-year-old daughter not only had a beeper, but a nearly-new usually bent-up Dodge Daytona with an automatic pilot to guide it into the body shop owned by her lover. You put it into your column. Some low-life publisher or producer with a wad of bills calls you up, pays you even more. Everyone makes out."

"Everyone but the readers," I said.

"It's the readers who want this stuff," he reminded me. "They'll read scandal before they'll read about poverty and the health care crisis."

"That may be true," I said, "but I'll pass on this one. My readers will just have to remain ignorant of the life of an obsessed teen and her sleazy adulterer."

"Don't come crying to me when 'Hard Copy' scoops you, and your editors replace you with someone known as 'a highly reliable source.'" I said I'd have to risk it. "By the way," Marshbaum said shortly before hanging up, "I'm sure you'll get a column out of this somehow. I'll send you a bill in the morning."

Piety requires us to honor truth above our friends.

Aristotle

Can a Columnist Have 'Friends'?

A columnist is something special. At least it feels that way when people recognize you. Sometimes the reaction is friendliness. Sometimes it's fear. If you write about local happenings, it's natural that big wigs and honchos want to fall on the good side of your pen.

Then some facts come your way that warrant a scathing exposé of a city council member whose kid is on the same soccer team as your son. Maybe a member of your Rotary Club is very friendly to you, but unfit for public office. With elections coming up, you have information to justify an unflattering profile.

When writing about people you may otherwise like, creating negative press can be tough duty. Accept it — people under criticism are sure to take personal offense.

Stu Bykofsky of the *Philadelphia Daily News* has punched out hard-hitting columns for 20 years. Witty, irascible, loved and loathed, his work is powered by outrage, and he admits it does take its physical and psychological toll. Still, it's his job to inform the public.

"You have three choices: 1) turn a blind eye; 2) do it more gently than otherwise; or 3) damn the torpedoes, fuck you, full speed ahead.

"Number two is the worst option, pulling the punches. If you're going to pull the trigger, aim for a bulls eye," he advised columnists at a 2005 NSNC meeting in Texas.

Expect to be shunned, blackballed, and hated. Powerful people react badly to a spotlight on their wrongdoings.

"In my column I've been on more shit lists than Scott bath-

155

room tissue. As long as you're being fair don't worry about those people putting obstacles in your path. It probably means you're doing your job right," says Bykofsky.

Attack: Professional vs. Personal

Not every columnist employs a full frontal assault. Each writer has an individual approach to dishing up criticism. One columnist might have a take-no-prisoners attitude. Another might pen a pointed but diplomatic disagreement. Humor might be another's weapon of choice. It is not a question of style, but the courage to present the facts. As Michael Corleone, a character in *The Godfather*, said, "It's not personal, Sonny. It's strictly business."

A columnist might be torn between the public's right to know and personal emotions. That being said, fairness requires accurate and complete reporting. Do not hold back any information or any efforts to uncover the truth. Always retain a defensible position from the vantage point of researched facts and reasoned argument. Criticism of someone's actions should not cross the line into personal attack.

Bykofsky applies his own "fairness test" to determine if his column strays into personal territory:

Insert your own name in the column.

Read it out loud and see how it feels.

Yes, it hurts, but is it accurate?

"If you wouldn't like somebody saying that about you with the same justification, then you might want to think about changing it," says Bykofsky.

Show Some Respect

Hardball writing is not exclusive to editorial or metro beat columnists. Any type of column involving criticism can generate enemies. Respect and accurate reporting strengthens a columnist's position.

"You can take somebody on and criticize them in a way that even they would admit was fair. You can't tear a person down," says columnist Maura Casey of *The New York Times*.

Robin Givhan covers style for *The Washington Post* and part of her job is to critique new fashion lines or to write about designers. At times, her review columns are pointedly unfavorable.

"You have to be aware of how you criticize someone with whom you have an ongoing professional relationship. The thing that upsets people about a bad review is if it's personal or disrespectful of their work. No matter if I think something stinks, the person who put it on the runway worked hard, has a passion and believed in it. If you're a columnist on a beat and you have to give a thumbs up or thumbs down, you have to remember to be respectful of the work," says Givhan.

Avoid hateful escalation, even in the face of vehement disagreement from others. A 2006 Pulitzer Prize winner for criticism, Givhan shared her own ground rules for doing reviews.

"Find your voice and a way to comfortably be opinionated but not overbearing.

"I write about things people make a conscious decision about — clothing, hair, or makeup. I don't write about physical features, body shape, bad skin, or wrinkles. Those are out of bounds because you have no control over things like that.

"Make sure your argument is measured and thoughtful, so that even if someone disagrees with you they can see how you got to it on your end. They can later rip your logic apart, but at least there are steps they can see you've taken," advises Givhan.

Humor columnists use laughter as a way of pointing out uncomfortable truths. Is everyone fair game?

One rule Dave Barry abides by is that he won't make fun of the defenseless.

"I pick on people who can fight back," he said before the 2006 Erma Bombeck Writers' Workshop in Dayton.

He was placed on an enemies list when North Dakota wanted to improve its image by changing the state's name to Dakota and he wrote a column mocking the effort.

"The folks in Grand Forks, North Dakota dedicated a sewage lift station to me. It's the Dave Barry Sewage Lift Station No.16 and a proclamation compared my work to human excrement," he laughed.

In taking pot shots, should any subjects be taboo?

"I don't think rape or the Holocaust or 9/11 is funny, but you can write around the edges of something. Like 9/11 is not funny but what happened to airline transportation security is," said Barry.

Hatred Close to Home

By Dave Lieber's reckoning, his exposés as a columnist for the *Fort Worth Star Telegram* have gotten many people into trouble or removed from positions. Around town, when he runs into such people, he reports the encounters are cordial. Despite being featured in an unflattering column, his subjects are treated with dignity, respect, and fairness, and most of the people he's written about recognize that.

"I don't call them names or mock them and I have always given them an opportunity to tell their side before I go to publication," says Lieber.

However, sometimes the anger and bitterness does not subside and can spill over toward the columnist's family. Lieber recalled a case when his reporting resulted in the ouster of a school superintendent in the district where Lieber's children attended school.

"There are some in the school district who will never forgive me. So I teach my children that their daddy had to stand up for freedom of the press and I had to do my job to remove someone who was apparently breaking state laws with his behavior.

"When the kids feel repercussions, and they usually do in school, you teach them to go with the flow and explain why it's happening — small-minded people are brainwashed into believing their fearless leader was wonderful. If he was so wonderful, why isn't he here anymore?" says Lieber.

What Happened To Everybody?

Just as subjects of an unflattering column may say to the writer, "I thought you were my friend," there may come a time when a columnist might ask the same question of others.

This happens when a columnist drops from view. Maybe a column is cancelled or the run dates are reduced. Perhaps the writer might draw a different assignment within the newspaper. Suddenly, all the attention is gone — the invitations, the emails, the phone calls — poof!

"I thought they were my friends," you might say.

Bykofsky offers a reality check:

"Most of the people you encounter aren't bad people, but they want your platform for their own ends. And that's fine as long as you understand you are in a business relationship. They will be with you as long as your business and their business coincide, but once you can no longer be of use to them, you're history."

He shared a valuable experience about "friends."

"Years ago, I was features editor of *The Daily News*, and I was on every guest list in town. There wasn't an opening or party I wasn't invited to. After two and half years, I got yanked off that job and shipped off to the night copy desk.

"It was like I had entered the gulag. I became a non-person. I was hurt. I felt bad that I'd been deserted by my so-called friends, but it taught me a lesson.

"They were inviting my title to those parties. They were not inviting me.

"Years later I got my column and I knew what to expect and I created a wall between what my column was, who I am, and who my friends were," says Bykofsky.

Often, keeping the professional distinct from the personal requires the mindset of an eight-armed Hindu goddess. So keep it simple. You already know who your real friends are and they probably don't ask to be featured in your column. As a columnist, a job well done requires telling the whole truth. Sometimes it makes people mad. You might be feared or even hated. But what counts is that you are respected.

Section 4:
What Lies Beyond the Column

Oh, the Places You'll Go
With a Column

By Deb DiSandro

For over 15 years, Deb DiSandro, a professional speaker and self-syndicated columnist, has coached writers and helped columnists to market beyond the column. She wrote two e-books, "So You Want to Be Columnist," and "Yes, You Can Write Funnier." She is the author of Tales of a Slightly Off Supermom (Pelican, 2003). A humorist, she gives presentations on Slightly Off success strategies for living.

Here DiSandro shares ideas and suggestions for broadening the appeal of a column as well as creating new opportunities.

One of my favorite books for dreaming big is Dr. Seuss' "Oh the Places You'll Go." As a columnist, I've found this message especially relevant, which is why I titled my last seminar, "Oh, the Places You'll Go with a Column." It may sound like an oxymoron, but to really reap the benefits of being a columnist, you must think and go beyond the column. Think further and go further than you've ever thunk before!

Your column is only the beginning of the exciting journey that lies ahead for you. When I penned the first Slightly Off column back in 1990, it was simply the name of the humor column that I hoped to syndicate one day. Sixteen years later, Slightly Off is the name of my business and my brand. It's the foundation for everything I do in my career.

When we first begin as columnists, we're usually focused on two main goals — getting our columns published in a newspaper and then, getting our column syndicated across the country. And yet, if we dig deeper, we may find that our true purpose goes beyond this narrow scope and vision.

Here are two questions worth asking, early on:

"What is the purpose of my column?"

"What do I want to accomplish with my column?"

These questions can open up a whole new world and change your perceptions about what you do and the direction you decide to take.

For me, the answer was, "I want to make people laugh." But more importantly, in getting people to laugh at me and my mistakes, I wanted them to see themselves and know that they are not alone. After hearing my stories, I wanted people to breathe a deep sigh of relief and say, "Wow! At least I'm not that dysfunctional!"

Notice I used the word "people" and not "readers"? This simple shift alone expands your direction. Now you can look for other avenues, in addition to your column, to reach people with your message. You can create a website, to share your vision and post columns. You can offer articles on your topic to magazines and e-zines. You can create presentations for audiences, businesses and organizations. You can write a book. You can offer segments to radio and TV stations. You can produce your own show and market it to the public. You can create your own products and services. My expanded vision allowed me to accomplish all this and more.

If you think in terms of purpose and fulfilling a need, you can become a sought after expert in your field. Jim Miller is the creator of "The Savvy Senior" (www.savysenior.org), a question and answer column offering resources for senior citizens. After assisting his own parents through many of life's senior hurdles, he saw a need for resources and information geared towards this burgeoning age group. When Jim began to self-syndicate the column, his purpose was to reach as many seniors as possible with the resources they needed. Because his vision was clear, Jim says he chose to offer his column at a "Wal-mart price." He didn't want price to be the reason a newspaper rejected his column. Today Savvy Senior is in over 400 newspapers. And Jim has definitely become a sought after expert in his field. He has a regular segment on the NBC Today show and recently appeared on CNBC!

Going beyond the column has worked for many businesses. Although "Ask the Builder" columnist Tim Carter began as a self-syndicator, six years later, when approached by Tribune

Media Services, he accepted their offer.

"I went with them as it freed me up to do other things," he says. Carter's column appears in 100+ papers. His website is a great example of how a columnist can take his columnist credibility and turn it into other streams of income.

"I make far more money from my website than I do from the newspapers that carry my column," Carter says, adding that 24,000 visitors a day visit his website, www.askthebuilder.com. Besides the advertisers on his site, Jim has created e-books.

When selecting a column topic and focus, select a name or title that defines your business. Often that name will be more memorable than your own! This is usually the best way to address your website — www.slightlyoff.com. When we think of building, Tim wants you to think ... Ask the Builder. When we need advice for seniors, Jim wants you to think ... The Savvy Senior. When I created the column title, Slightly Off, not only did I have a unique name for a humor column, but I had unknowingly created a brand, and a philosophy of life! I have become an expert in Slightly Off Strategies for reducing stress and finding more happiness in everyday life. My mission is to help people let go of the super syndrome and embrace their Slightly Off side.

In my Slightly Off Seminars, I have also created characters that reflect my brand: Dr. Slightly Off, the wise and witty doctor with the Slightly Off prescription, and the Slightly Off Supermom — a healthier, happier version of supermom with a Slightly Off style all her own. This brand was also used in my book, *Tales of a Slightly Off Supermom: Fighting for Truth, Justice and Clean Underwear.*

Yes, I am a columnist, but I'm Slightly Off first!

So, go ahead, and imagine where your column may take you. Enjoy the journey! Here are some tips to get you started:

■ When establishing your column, know your purpose or overall goal for reaching the public.

■ Make sure that your column fills a need — instead of just offering the column, you might also provide resources and information for your targeted audience.

■ Become an expert in your field.

■ Explore the many ways you can reach your audience; speaking, products, radio, television, seminars, specialty gifts.

■ Find a hook, a unique way of presenting your message — something that distinguishes you from the crowd.

■ Use your column credibility as an avenue to other venues.

■ Choose a business name or brand that reflects your message.

Anyone writing newspaper columns for the money should probably be classified as a fictional character.

W. Bruce Cameron

Syndication

Syndication — the very word evokes a Mount-Everest-type of awe from the aspiring. One fervently hopes someday to scale that mighty peak. At least that's the buzz back at base camp: "How do I get syndicated?" "What are they looking for?" "Whom should I contact?"

Before donning crampons for the long, cold trek upward, let's be clear on the quest.

Self-Syndication

Self-syndication is when a freelance columnist sells, markets, and manages his/her own work, and the advantage is full artistic and financial control. The disadvantage might be that more energy is spent on marketing and administration than on writing. Also, distribution and resulting revenues are limited to one's personal efforts.

Undaunted self-syndicators may forge ahead with ideas and advice found elsewhere in this guide.

This chapter focuses on third-party syndication, that is, a business entity that is responsible for the sale and distribution of work created by others for publication. Here are two main examples of syndication:

The Traditional Syndicate

The moneyed way is through an established syndicate, which provides content for publication in newspapers and other media. A number of traditional syndicates post submission guidelines on their Web sites. A list appears at the end of this chapter, so keep your crampons on.

If accepted by a syndicate, a columnist will enter into a contract for exclusive representation. Syndication representatives will market the columnist's work to newspapers and content outlets and sale proceeds traditionally are split 50/50 between the syndicate and columnist.

How much can a column fetch? The syndicate charges anywhere from $3 to $300 per subscribing newspaper, according to Rick Newcombe, president of Creators Syndicate. So the columnist's take is half that.

The circulation of a newspaper is the basis for fees. The larger the newspaper, the more it has to pay for a syndicated column, generally speaking.

Typically, fees are based on "historical precedent," that is, what the customer has paid for content in the past. But sometimes a special columnist can command higher fees.

"It can be as high as $600 for Ann Landers but that was very unusual," says Newcombe, who founded Creators Syndicate in 1987.

But running in hundreds of newspapers doesn't happen overnight, if ever, any more.

W. Bruce Cameron, author of the bestseller *8 Simple Rules for Dating My Teenage Daughter* (Workman, 2002), signed on with Creators Syndicate in 2001.

That same year another syndicated humorist, Tony Kornheiser, retired and Cameron was slated to fill that slot with 50 newspapers. The expectation was that Cameron's syndication would grow to 200 newspapers in a few years.

But the national tragedy on September 11, 2001, changed everything, and one lesser by-product was the unwillingness by many newspapers to fill humor vacancies.

So Cameron's 2001 syndication instead began with seven newspapers, and now his column runs in 50. Even for the syndicated, a slow climb continues.

"One must have a couple dozen large circulation newspapers, or a hundred or more medium-sized ones, before there is any noticeable impact on the bottom line. Self-syndication is far more practical for a person with fewer than a dozen newspapers," advises Cameron.

Traditional syndication offers the advantage of simultaneous submission, with access to hundreds of publications. Also, the syndicate handles everything: marketing, distribution, billing, collection, and payment to the writer.

In 2007 Media Matters for America collected data on syndicated columnists from almost every daily newspaper. Part of its study examined "The Top Ten Columnists By Number of Newspapers." The study's focus was on daily newspapers.

Conservative columnist George Will was ranked No. 1 with his columns carried in 328 dailies. In comparison, the No. 10 spot was held by centrists Cokie and Steven Roberts, who co-author a column that is syndicated in 49.

Dave Barry's humor column ran in over 500 newspapers, but today that level of syndication is rare.

Syndication Through a Newspaper Chain

This is the less moneyed way. A family of newspapers may be owned or managed by a conglomerate, which forms its own news service syndicate. Such a syndicate may share content among its member papers, including columns. Thus, a columnist may write for a particular paper, but his/her column may run in any of the chain's other newspapers. Often the writer will not receive additional compensation and is precluded contractually from working with a traditional syndicate as well. No riches here, but the advantage is wider circulation, an increased readership, and a chance to open other doors.

Syndication is not automatic for columnists who are featured in a member paper owned by a newspaper chain. Such columnists should ask the editor they work with about the possibilities. Or contact a fellow columnist who is syndicated with the chain and ask for guidance.

Enough. The head spinning in *Exorcist* couldn't keep up with all the confusing aspects of syndication. So let's leave it with the above basics and get into a more compelling question, which is, how can the syndication spotlight shine on you?

Breaking Into Syndication

Breaking in sounds like we first need to huddle in Tony Soprano's basement. And isn't it a crime that you're not syndicated?

So let's say you follow a traditional syndicate's on-line guidelines and submit sample columns to them. What are your chances of getting picked up?

Using Creators Syndicate as an example, the odds would be 1 in about 1,000.

"We receive about 7,000 submissions a year and we'll bring out three new columnists and three new cartoonists," said Newcombe.

Odds are slim but not impossible. As you plan to scale the syndicate mountain, again review honestly your goals: What do you want really your column to do? For whom are you writing and who is your target audience?

What, What, What Do They Want?

What makes a columnist stand out in the eyes of a syndicate? Newcombe shares insights on deciding factors:

■ Someone who can provide information not found from another source

■ Great writing

■ Brilliant analysis

■ A proven readership, i.e. a best-selling author or a newspaper's most popular columnist

■ A big name

Robert C. Koehler is a 12-year editor with Tribune Media Services. An award-winning journalist for 30 years, Koehler writes a syndicated column, "Common Wonders," which he describes as "Part Political Brawl. Part Secular Prayer." At Tribune Media Services, Koehler has been editor to Arianna Huffington and the late Art Buchwald, among others.

"The best syndicated writers judiciously push the envelope," he says.

Koehler agrees that a popular columnist with a large following does increase his/her syndication possibilities. Like newspapers, syndicate houses are undergoing rapid changes in the industry. It's natural to lean toward the tried and true. The growth of the Internet as well as economic forces seen in the mergers and divisions of communication companies also has made an impact on newspaper content.

"They [the syndicates] have far less interest in developing markets for talented unknowns, especially in the realm of general commentary," says Koehler.

The 2007 study by Media Matters For America reported, "Sixty percent of the nation's daily newspapers print more conservative syndicated columnists every week than progressive syndicated columnists."

At Tribune Media Services, Koehler observed, "Political commentary is about half of what we syndicate. The other half are various niches: health, travel, gossip, horoscope, etc., and a few lifestyle/humor columns."

So is your work doomed if you write more about pets than politics?

Surprisingly, Koehler feels luck can be more the deciding factor in getting syndicated than genius prose.

"National syndication has more to do with luck and knowing the right people or being in the right place at the right time than just the sheer quality of writing. It helps to be good but it's not strictly necessary. If only attaining a certain level of prose quality automatically opened the door.

"I read lots of excellent writers who are not syndicated and lots of mediocre ones who are. Who will be given a shot of syndication? Once syndicated, who will succeed and be a hit with editors? It's a mystery," says Koehler.

Certainly, W. Bruce Cameron says, "I was very, very lucky." Years ago, he appeared on a radio show, and host Oliver North, the former White House aide, asked him if a syndication company distributed his column.

"When I admitted that I had tried and failed to obtain one, he promised to write a letter to the president of Creators, which he faithfully did. With that sort of in, my column was passed out to editors from the president's office, and I wound up being syndicated," recalls Cameron. (Note: In 2006, Cameron won both the Robert Benchley Award for Best Humorist and the National Society of Newspaper Columnists Award for Best Humor Columnist. It's not all luck.)

Syndication should not be viewed as the ultimate goal in column writing, but rather, a valuable tool for career advancement. The TV series based on Cameron's *8 Simple Rules For Dating My Teenage Daughter* followed in 2002 after his syndication with Creators. Now his new book, *8 Simple Rules For Marrying My Daughter*, will be published in 2008.

"With each book I publish, I have a broader fan base, and also it seems to help Creators sell my column to more papers. So syndication — when viewed as part of the three-legged stool of my writing career — holds a very important place in the overall strategy.

"The three-legged stool upon which I am sitting while I try to milk the cow of success is composed of columns, books, and movies/television. The stool wobbles and I keep falling off it and landing in cow poop," says Cameron.

Here he suggests ways to approach syndicate houses:

■ Try the personal approach over blind submissions.

■ Approach syndicated columnists you know and request an introduction.

■ Or if you work for a newspaper, the editors probably know the syndicate's representative. Get his or her name and number.

Also, Dave Astor *of Editor & Publisher* magazine (www.editorandpublisher.com) keenly covers syndication topics. Look for his print and on-line reports. For smaller, newer, regional, and specialty syndicates, consult *The Editor & Publisher Directory of Syndicated Services.*

Finally, let's not forget that new communication forms are expanding the need for content. Columnists are essential to a syndicate's success.

"We're not in the newspaper business, we're in the content business, and so a lot of our new business is coming from new media — iPods, cell phones, the Internet. Our goal is to find the very best content. Our assets are the columnists and cartoonists that we represent," says Newcombe.

And for those who never get syndicated?

Koehler says, "The Internet creates instant opportunity for a forum, and it's a healthy challenge to the traditional media, but it's not a moneymaker in and of itself. Still, it certainly amplifies a person's voice and creates the chance to reach many people, bypassing syndication altogether."

The Syndicates and the Web: Where to Find Submission Guidelines

By Ben S. Pollock with Dan St. Yves

Listings excerpted from the National Society of Newspaper Columnists Syndication Guide. Used with permission.

Canadian Artists Syndicate, includes Miller Features Syndicate
www.artistsyndicate.ca/, with guidelines linked on index at left.

Copley News Service
www.copleynews.com/copleynews/navigation/default.asp, and guidelines at www.copleynews.com/copleynews/FrontPage/Submissions.htm

Creators Syndicate
www.creators.com/, and guidelines at www.creators.com/submissions.html

King Features
www.kingfeatures.com, and guidelines at www.kingfeatures.com/subg_column.htm

The New York Times Syndicate
www.nytsyn.com/syndicate.html, but no online guidelines

Tribune Media Services
www.tmsfeatures.com/tmsfeatures/maincategory.jsp?catid=23 and guidelines at www.tmsfeatures.com/submissions.html

United Media (United Feature Syndicate and Newspaper Enterprise Association [NEA])
www.unitedfeatures.com/ufsapp/home.do and guidelines at www.unitedfeatures.com/ufs/submissions.html

Universal Press Syndicate (Andrews McMeel Universal)
www.uexpress.com/ and guidelines at www.amuniversal.com/ups/submissions.htm

Washington Post Writers Group
postwritersgroup.com/writersgroup.htm and guidelines at www.postwritersgroup.com/submissionguidecolumn.html

For smaller, newer, regional, and specialty syndicates, consult *The Editor & Publisher Directory of Syndicated Services* — available from large libraries and at www.editorandpublisher.com/eandp/resources/syndicate.jsp.

Consult the most recent edition available as some of these organizations are relatively short-lived.

The above are syndicates as commonly defined, not news services. The broadest news services include the Associated Press and Reuters. They generally do not accept free-lance columns, except possibly through member or subscribing newspapers.

Other news services belong to newspaper conglomerates. These supplemental news services of newspaper chains distribute within and beyond their papers only columns written by employees. As a rule they do not syndicate freelancers, except perhaps those contracted by a member newspaper individually. Those then might be distributed in the service. If your column already is published by a newspaper owned by a chain, ask your editor there for information.

These news services include:

Gannett News Service, www.gannett.com/web/news-papers.htm

Los Angeles Times-Washington Post News Service, www.newsservice.com/

McClatchy-Tribune Information Services (marketed by Tribune Media Services and formerly Knight-Ridder/Tribune Information Services), www.mctdi-rect.com/shared/mct.htm

Newhouse News Service, www.newhouse.com/about-newhouse-news-service.html

The New York Times News Service, www.nytsyn.com/newsservice.html

Scripps Howard News Service (marketed by United Media, part of E.W. Scripps Co.), www.shns.com/shns/g_index2.cfm?action=home

Web designers always are fine-tuning, and site addresses such as these may expire. You can type into an Internet search engine the full name of the syndication company and "column submission guidelines."

Each friend represents a world in us, a world not born until they arrive, and it is only by this meeting that a new world is born.

Anais Nin

Blogging

Weblogs or blogs have gained exponential momentum. The immediate posting of news and opinions on such public journals has leveled the playing field between professional columnists and avocationists.

The blogosphere is a lightning-fast posting realm of on-the-spot news and commentary. It is a cyber mecca for those seeking to shine light into secrets and uncover truths, as well as a place of outrageous claims and self-centered rants. Effective blogging structures and forms continue to evolve.

One columnist, Arianna Huffington, has transformed the blogosphere by pushing innovation toward its full expression. Nationally syndicated with Tribune Media Services, she also is the co-host of *Left, Right and Center*, public radio's political round-table program. Her eleventh book, *On Becoming Fearless in Love, Work and Life*, was published in 2006.

On May 9, 2005, she co-founded the *Huffington Post*, www.huffingtonpost.com, a blog/news site featuring over 750 writers. One year later, HuffPost was drawing 2.6 million unique viewers a month and generating 24 million page views, according to a 2006 interview with *Editor & Publisher*.

At the 2006 annual meeting of the National Society of Newspaper Columnists in Boston, Huffington shared six hard-won insights into the success of *Huffington Post*:

Six Online Rules

By Arianna Huffington
(Keynote excerpts, July 1, 2006)

Here are my first six rules about the online universe:

Rule One

It's not either/or. This whole debate about the future of journalism — is it print or is it online — is a completely irrelevant, old-fashioned obsolete debate, as obsolete as the old Ginger vs. Mary Ann barroom argument. I say it's 2006. Let's have a three-way.

It's not either/or. There is no question that in the course of our lifetime and our children's lifetime, both print and online are going to be forces. The question is how can print not just survive, but thrive in this brave new world?

I have two teenage daughters, 15 and 17. My 17-year-old wants to be a journalist, and she does most of her reading online; she even watches "Desperate Housewives" and "Law and Order" on her laptop — even though she has a perfectly good plasma TV in my office she can go to — because that's how this generation is used to operating. But at the same time, every week she buys five or six magazines on top of all the ones I subscribe to. And when I offered her an internship at the *Huffington Post* or at *Slate* through my friends there, or at *Salon.com,* she says, "No mom, I'd rather intern at a print magazine." And in fact, she's starting on Wednesday interning at *Vanity Fair.* So this is really part of what a lot of young people are doing. Even though they're moving online, they are still gravitating towards print.

At the same time, remember, there is 68 percent of readers who don't read online at all. I love the online universe, but let's not exaggerate the significance in terms of where print is going to be in the course of our lifetime.

Rule Two

My second ground rule that I've learned the hard way is that if it ain't porn, don't charge for it. Basically the idea of *The New York Times,* that you put your best content behind a wall, is just so missing the whole point of the online universe. So unless it's porn or sports, or financial services, do not even think of charging.

Trust advertising to be a source of revenue.

At the moment, only 5 percent of advertising expenditures is spent online, but it's growing at the rate of 28 percent a year. We at the *Huffington Post* expected to start attracting advertisers after a year, but we were attracting advertising after three months. Now we are actually profitable entirely through advertising. So it is a phenomenon, and you can take advantage of it online.

Advertisers are looking at many ways to make advertising more interesting, not just an interaction of content, but to make it part of content, while observing the Berlin Wall between editorial and advertising.

At a recent advertising convention I attended, there were over 8,000 advertisers from all around the world, and they are much more terrified than print people are about the future of advertising. They have to deal with TiVo, they have to deal with the fact that readers are becoming much more selective and they don't want to have things like ads imposed on them, so this is the time when they're gravitating to the online universe.

Rule Three

My third lesson that I've learned is that online readers are not your father's readers — and the same goes for print. Readers want to be engaged. They want to be involved. They don't want just to listen — they want to be heard. It's like a relationship. Imagine being in a relationship where only one person does the talking. How long can it last?

It's not going to last forever, right? So it's very important to engage our readers, to make the relationship interactive. Our readers, we have found in the *Huffington Post*, are commentors, they are editors, they are fact checkers, they're reporters, and they're just amazing. I'm stunned by the comments on the *Huffington Post* and we are investing a lot of resources in moderating the comments. We don't want our community taken over by trolls, which is one of the problems of the Internet. We want comments, but we don't want unmoderated comments.

We have dozens of volunteers and staffers helping this community grow. It is an amazing community. Anybody who has worked with commentors knows just how incredibly valuable they are. You make a mistake in your post and it's going to be caught within seven seconds. Literally. Giving readers the power to actually find mistakes and be able to report and edit is just one of the great treasures of being online.

Rule Four

My fourth rule has to do with the fact that increasingly readers/users want their news as well as their commentary to be instant. We have over 750 bloggers who are given a password and they can comment on anything that's happening. What works for the *Huffington Post* is that we have 24-7 news, together with constant opinion and commentary, and not just on things that are immediate, but also on long-term issues.

Last July I remember waking up and seeing the front page of *The New York Times* with a picture of jubilant Londoners celebrating the fact they got the Olympics. Then I watched CNN and saw the horrific pictures of the subway bombing that took place shortly afterwards. On the *Huffington Post* was a fantastic blog post from Simon Jenkins, who until recently was the editor of *The Evening Sun*, offering real-time, on-site commentary on what was happening in London.

This is the world that we are living in. You'd better have an online presence that updates what is happening. It's not every day, of course, that two major international events happen within 48 hours so that your front page becomes obsolete by the time your readers have woken up, but it's an indication of how we need to be in real time with what is happening.

Rule Five

My fifth ground rule is: don't fall into the access trap. Bob Woodward was part of the creation of investigative journalism for the new generation, and then he fell into the access trap. It's a terrible trap for journalists, because basically you trade in your journalistic pass for an all-access pass.

So there he was. He had this unprecedented access to the White House and this administration during the lead-up to the war. You read his book, *Plan of Attack*, and you miss the whole story. There is all this detail that he got from being on the scene but missing the big story, which is that this country was misled into war. That's really what we need to guard against more than anything.

The greatest value of the blogosphere for me is the fact that you have people who are not trading on access. A lot of them have no access at all, but that can be an advantage because you're not afraid to step on any toes, or afraid that you're not going to be invited to the White House Christmas party, or that you're not going to be part of the social scene in Washington, which is what self-censors so many journalists. What the blogosphere has been for the mainstream media is incredibly healthy. It's really keeping the mainstream media's feet to the fire.

And at the same time let us not underestimate the significance of the mainstream media in breaking stories. I've been a major critic of *The New York Times* over the last year, over Judy Miller, but this is a time to celebrate *The New York Times*. I made a list of all the breaking stories by U.S. media, stories that we would not have known about because this is the most secretive administration in history. The war on terror and 9/11 are being used to prevent us from knowing things that are incredibly important to our national security.

We would not have known about Abu Ghraib were it not for *The New Yorker* and Sy Hersh. We would not have known about Haditha if it were not for *Time* magazine. The secret prison system that is operating, we would not have known about if it were not for *The Washington Post*. The fact that the president has 750 signed statements that somehow make it possible for him to ignore bills that he has signed into law, we would not have known about without *The Boston Globe*. The fact that Alberto Gonzales considers the Geneva Convention quaint, we would not have known about without *Newsweek*. The fact that 50,000 Iraqis have died since the beginning of the war we would not have known about without *The Los Angeles Times*. The fact that Dick Cheney was intimately involved in Plamegate we would not have known without Murray Waas of *The National Journal*. He is one of the great investigative journalists/bloggers who go back and forth between the print and online worlds.

Rule Six

My sixth rule focuses on the main distinguishing difference between the blogosphere and mainstream media.

The mainstream media suffer from ADD — attention deficit disorder, that is, they write about a story and then they move on.

We find that unless you stay with a story, and stay with a story, and stay with a story, it doesn't break through the static.

Many, many major stories have died on the front pages of *The New York Times*. It's not that these stories are not covered, it's that they are not covered obsessively.

We in the blogosphere are suffering from OCD, obsessive-compulsive disorder.

We pick up a story and don't let it go.

I remember when I was writing about the war on drugs regularly, because I believe it's one of the great disasters of American domestic policy. My editor would call and say you wrote about that last month, or you wrote about that three months ago, depending on their tolerance level. I would say yes, but I'm bringing you new facts and new information. It's the same topic, but new developments.

But no, the mainstream media don't like that. They want you to keep writing about new things, new issues.

In the blogosphere we have shown how you can engage your readers by staying with a story, and it almost becomes like a great serial, right? You give them the next installment and the next installment. People want to know what's happening next, like a child listening to a story.

So to return to my first point, it is not either/or. It's both print and online. I say you've got ADD. We've got OCD. Together we can be crazy effective.

— Arianna Huffington

You see, wire telegraph is a kind of a very, very long cat. You pull his tail in New York and his head is meowing in Los Angeles. Do you understand this? And radio operates exactly the same way: you send signals here, they receive them there. The only difference is that there is no cat.

Albert Einstein, when asked to describe radio

Radio: On the Air With Columnists

Are you curious how a columnist can break into radio? On Radio Road, two writers have expanded their careers in opposite directions. Columnist Margery Eagan of *The Boston Herald* has reported metro happenings since 1989, which led to guest commentary on radio shows. Since 1999, in addition to her newspaper column, Eagan co-hosts a Boston radio talk show with Jim Braude on 96.9 FM Talk, Eagan and Braude, which covers wide-ranging issues.

Broadcaster Mike Morin has been a radio personality for 36 years in Washington, D.C., New York City, and Boston. Now working in Manchester, New Hampshire, Morin currently hosts the state's highest rated morning show at 95.7-WZID. In 2000 he was named New Hampshire's Radio Personality of the Year by the N.H. Association of Broadcasters. In 2004 Morin began writing a newspaper humor column, which appears weekly in *The Nashua Telegraph*. In 2006 he became a monthly columnist for *New Hampshire Business Review*.

Here Margery Eagan shares how her metro column launched her into radio:

Q: *Describe the type of column you write.*

ME: I've been a *Boston Herald* columnist for 17 years. My col-

179

umn is very much off the news. I cover lots of trials, elections. Occasionally I do lifestyle, softer stuff. For example, I did a piece about beauty wars.

Q: *How long had you been writing a column before radio opportunities came up?*

ME: It might have been right away. Local radio stations call reporters a lot. I would get calls when they were interested in my subjects. Murder trials, news, elections, whatever was hot in the news that day.

Q: *What was it about your writing that sparked interest in you as a possible radio show host?*

ME: What makes a good columnist is that you want to write about what people are talking about and the same is true of radio.

Q: *Had you had any prior radio experience before becoming a columnist?*

ME: None.

Q: *What were some challenges for you in adapting to a radio format?*

ME: It's hard to do it by yourself. At first, as a fill-in host, I was alone and I had to talk by myself. Boston has a lot of competition and a bigger market is harder. Radio is just like a column in that it's obvious very quickly if you're going to be any good at it.

Q: *How long have you co-hosted 96.9 FM Talk with Jim Braude?*

ME: Seven years.

Q: *What types of columns might open the door to radio possibilities?*

ME: Political analysis, exposés, crime reporting, sports. There's a lot of crossover between newspaper columns and radio work.

Q: *What kind of qualities or skills does a columnist need to break into radio?*

ME: Everyone who has succeeded in the big time is incredibly smart.

Also, here in Boston there seems to be a big difference in the way men and women in radio are received. The public is more accepting of abrasiveness in male hosts, and yet with women, it matters if listeners like you. It's a double standard.

Almost no women do radio alone, but one exception is Laura Ingraham who is incredibly smart and does well.

My observation, at least here in Boston, is that a woman might do better if she co-hosts with a man. My co-host is very smart and quit-witted, but he can be abrasive. It's easier for me to play off of him. It appears harder for a woman to be confrontational and succeed. Also, for whatever reason, I've observed that two female co-hosts together never seems to work. Maybe it's that double standard again.

Longtime broadcaster Mike Morin shares his insider's view on parlaying a column into on-air time:

Q: *What does a radio station look for in a columnist?*

MM: It's very helpful for a writer to come across the same as he or she does in print. Radio listeners can detect phoniness. He or she should have the same "voice" so as to not disappoint the listener. A great speaking voice isn't a requisite, but avoiding lots of "ums" and "ahs" is important. Speak with confidence. You're opinionated. That should be reflected in a friendly way in your tone.

My 36 years in radio was great training for column writing, because economy of word usage is important. Streamline your thoughts but be conversational. Don't take detours to make your point. Often, less is more on radio as you are competing with many distractions and listeners need you to get to the point before the baby starts to fuss or their cell phone rings.

Q: *What kinds of columnists typically get invited by stations to be on the air?*

MM: In our area (Boston), the greatest demand seems to be for sports writers on the city's all-sports station, WEEI. Many are paid nicely to serve as guests.

Several have done so well they now have their own shows. *Boston Herald* muckraking columnist and mob expert Howie Carr makes a pile of money hosting the afternoon drive daily on WRKO. General humor writers might get a call from morning radio shows if they write something that sparks lively conversation on their shows.

You should be sure morning DJs have your phone number so they can wake you from a deep sleep to talk about your morning column. If you're really good, you could get invited to be an in-studio guest sometime and who knows, maybe even more.

Q: *Is it helpful if a columnist is an "expert" or if the columnist wrote a book?*

MM: Being an expert or author might be good for a one shot invitation. If you are an expert on plants, you might find a weekly spot Saturday morning fielding calls for gardeners. Food experts can be in demand around holidays.

Don't be shy about letting local radio hosts and their producers know that you're available for on-air segments.

Psychology, medical, lifestyle stuff — think in terms of people's daily life needs. The more narrow your area of expertise, the less likely you'll be called. Chances are a writer who knows a lot about toilet tank floats is destined to keep that information to himself. Sad, huh?

Q: *If a columnist is an author, what person at a station should he/she contact and how should the pitch be made?*

MM: Authors who do not have publicity representation should contact producers and hosts directly. Be sure you have an excellent one-page press release and be prepared to offer free review copies to the host and producer (if there is one).

Smaller markets do not have producers. The talent books guests and conducts the interviews. After a week or two, follow up with a polite email or call, inquiring if the material might be of interest for an interview segment.

Listen to the show for a few weeks first to determine the suitability of your material for the audience. It's just like a writing query — read the publication before you submit a manuscript. Sending a book on spiders to a political talk host is a waste of your good book.

Q: *Is there one person, generally, who makes the best all-around contact at a station?*

MM: I'd approach in this order:
   1. Producer

2. Host

3. Program Director

Q: *What experience/qualities/skills should a columnist pitch about him/herself to attract show time as a guest on a local station?*

MM: They should assure the producer/host that they can be available when needed. It's good to let them know that the book is selling well at the local bookstore and that reviews are very good.

Do not oversell a book. Be friendly, confident and willing to bend over backwards to accommodate a station's needs. I've had authors tell me to call them if I ever need a guest in a pinch. Really good guests are often contacted as "experts" when their area of knowledge is in the news. Maybe a big story on global warming is in the headlines. Talk shows go to their files to find the guy who was a great guest about how flatulent cows are a factor in global warming. Always be ready to help out. Guests cancel all the time and instant replacements are needed.

Q: *List five "baby steps" a columnist can take to get on the air.*

MM: 1. Accept that radio exposure will get more people to read your column.

2. Listen to local morning shows and other talk shows. Look for hosts who interview guests or experts.

3. If you write a column you think a certain host might like, email a link to him/her with a polite note saying you'd be available should the host have an interest in discussing your column with his/her listeners.

4. Attend functions that radio people attend. Introduce yourself and give them a business card. Follow up with a "nice to meet you" email a week later. Stay in touch but don't be a pest.

5. If the preceding four fail, bake them chocolate chip cookies wrapped in one of your columns.

Q: *If a columnist wanted to develop a radio show out of his/her readership following, how would they go about that? Is it done by proposal first, or do you have to have a demo tape prepared?*

MM: It's just like pitching a writing project. Begin by telling a program director why you believe your idea will be of interest to a station's audience. Research the station's demographics and be sure your idea matches THEIR core audience. A hard rock station will have no interest in a show about scrap booking.

Listen to the station and submit a format proposal, based on how you hear the station proceed with existing programs.

Send an overview, proposal, and sample show (script) to the program director.

Offer to do a studio demo, or better yet, offer to do several free shows so they can evaluate your potential and you can see if you're any good at it.

If your topic has to do with community interest, you might have a good chance since the FCC requires a certain amount of that type of programming weekly for a station to maintain its license. If you are a car expert, find a dealership or mechanic who will sponsor a weekly call-in segment. Take your expertise and find someone who will pay the way.

Q: *Lastly, Margery Eagan stated listeners are more accepting of on-air rudeness in men but not in women. Any thoughts?*

MM: Radio personalities have to be accepted by their audience. Start slowly and build equity with your audience. Don't bully them. If you do, be damned sure it's deserved.

Be yourself. After a while, listeners will consider you their friend. I have listeners who will bake for me, invite me to events, who want to date me. As far as guys being able to be more abrasive, that's true to some degree. But if you're a successful female writer with an edge, take it to the air and maintain that consistent "voice."

Dr. Laura can sound annoying at times, but is successful. Judge Judy is another example. They are true to themselves on the air and can get away with it. Once people begin to accept you, you'll be able to turn up the heat so slowly, no one will notice. Radio is a medium of personality nuances.

Laughter is the closest distance between two people.

Victor Borge

Journalism and Standup Comedy: There is a Difference

By Ray Hanania

Columnist and author Ray Hanania has two facets to his career. A veteran Chicago political reporter, his columns focus on Middle East and mainstream American issues. Separately, he tours nationally as a standup comedian.

Originally distributed by Creators Syndicate, Hanania now self-syndicates directly to major newspapers and new media. Hanania, a Palestinian American, was named "Best National Ethnic Columnist" in 2006 by the New America Media. He is the recipient of two Chicago Headline Club/Society of Professional Journalists' Lisagor Awards for Column Writing (1985, 2002/03). His columns are archived on www.hanania.com.

Hanania's Arab American-Jewish comedy routine lampoons his life and marriage to his wife, Alison, who is Jewish. He performs at clubs and universities and is the author of eight books, including the humor books "I'm Glad I Look Like a Terrorist: Growing Up Arab in America" and "Talking to Israelis."

Here, Hanania shares how political commentary evolved into including standup comedy in his career as a columnist.

It wasn't until after Sept. 11, 2001 and the terrorist attacks that day that I realized that good journalism alone was not enough to inform the uninformed American public.

It was the beginning of the expansion of my 30-year journalism career into standup comedy. It wasn't easy. But I had no

185

choice. For me, it was as much about professional survival as it was about physical survival.

Sept. 11 nearly destroyed my journalism career, cast me as a bad guy to most prospective media and especially to the public, and undermined my ability to earn a living.

I lost jobs. Made more enemies without even knowing it, and was "laid-off" in a company-wide downsizing, that downsized only one job. Mine.

Although today nearly half of my income comes from standup comedy performances around the country and the world, the transformation from journalist to journalist-comedian came wholly by accident.

I was attending a communications luncheon conference hosted by Columbia College in Chicago when two of my best friends approached me and asked, with straight faces and serious demeanor, "Why did your people attack us on Sept. 11?"

I could have addressed that question seriously, but I realized a question founded on a ridiculous premise could not be answered with a straightforward, reasoned, and rational comment.

So I started to just make jokes.

"My people?" I replied, "I'm from the South Side of Chicago. I know they're rough, but are we sure the terrorists are South Siders?"

The more they tried to get a serious answer, the more I responded with ridiculous, rough attempts at humor.

My friends laughed at my responses, prompting one to suggest that I take my impromptu routine and turn it into a standup comedy act.

Why not, I figured? Americans often really don't want truth. They prefer answers of convenience that fit their beliefs.

The Power of Humor

There is no serious answer to a stupid question. I had nothing to do with Sept. 11. I never heard of Osama Bin Laden or al-Qaeda, and more important, although I am Arab, I am Christian Palestinian and all the hijackers were Muslims, most from Saudi Arabia.

As a journalist, I've always used humor in my writing. Humor is the most effective form of communications. We use humor all the time, in the form of anecdotes to help "humanize" complex topics. Speakers are taught that the best way to capture an audience's attention is to begin with a good joke, even if the joke has nothing to do with the speech topic.

Humor is powerful. It can change attitudes, shatter stereotypes and break bonds of animosity.

In fact, the fundamental character of a "good joke" has more to do with the ability of the audience to quickly understand what the comedian is saying than the comedian's ability to stereotype and generalize complex issues.

You can have the best joke in the world but if the audience doesn't understand you, the joke will die.

Standup comedy is about "punch lines." Short, fast, machine-gun fired jokes. It's much tougher than simply adding humor to a long exposé on a serious societal topic.

I had no experience in writing standup comedy punch-line driven jokes. Most of my past use of humor involved writing lengthy funny stories to set the emotional mood for features, columns, and even a few news stories.

But I did have some experience. Most of my writing before Sept. 11 was about the serious side of the Middle East conflict, although occasionally I saw something funny that was worth exploring.

In 1988, I wrote a full-length feature for Chicago magazine on "growing up Arab in America" that was filled with humorous anecdotes I hoped would help the reader identify with the storied experience. The feature began, "My mother wanted me to become a doctor or a grocery store owner. I never knew I would grow up one day to become an Arab."

Years later, after the terrorist attack on the Murrah Federal Building in Oklahoma City, I used that feature, and about 30 other columns I had written on similar topics over the years including at the *Chicago Sun-Times* where I had won several awards for coverage of the city's tumultuous City Hall, to lead off a book on "growing up Arab in America" that I titled "I'm Glad I Look Like a Terrorist."

In investigating the Murrah Federal Building bombing, authorities focused on Arabs and only stumbled upon the real terrorist, a Scottish Christian. I realized that Americans were quick to jump to conclusions in part because Arab Americans have done a poor job presenting themselves to Americans as being very much like the immigrants who came to this country from Italy, Ireland, Poland, and who were Jews, African Americans, and Hispanics.

The controversial title was satire and it came from a *Sun-Times* column, which explored the silver lining of being an Arab American profiled every time I passed through an airport in the 1990s. Security officers would pull me out of the long and tedious customs lines and process me, discover I wasn't a threat, and help me avoid airport delays.

Famed radio host Casey Kassem, who is also Arab, wrote me urging me to change the title of the book to "I'm glad I don't look like a terrorist." I replied if I used that title, no one would read it.

Humor and satire, I said, is something Americans understand probably better than any other people in the world. Most, not all, would know what I was trying to say.

But the trauma of Sept. 11 was so great I had to do more. I set my sights on standup comedy. I realized there were only a dozen Arab Americans who were engaged in standup comedy, making it easy for me to fill a void.

Fundamentals of a Comedy Routine

In everyday life, we all know comedians. But what keeps them from being successful? Stage fright. Most of the funniest people I know are those we work with and share our social time with.

But put them on a stage? No way. They'd never make it.

My success came in part because I was pushed into the need to transition from professional journalism to standup comedy. Had it been a choice, I would never have taken the steps. It is interesting, I think, that reporters and columnists have different personalities. Reporters tend to have personalities best suited for behind-the-scenes. Columnists, on the other hand, have Type A personalities. They can't afford to shy away from conflict, the spotlight, or public debates.

That made it easier for me to go on stage and use my experience as a public speaker to also stand on stage in front of hundreds of people and tell jokes.

But I still had to come up with jokes.

I did what we all do. I looked back at my life and picked real stories that I streamlined, punched up, and highlighted the "contrast" that creates the "funny."

When I was a kid growing up on Chicago's South Side, the other kids surrounded me one day and asked, "What are you?"

"What am I? I'm an American," I said. No you're not, they insisted.

I finally went back to my dad and asked, "Dad, what am I?"

It was weeks after the 1967 war and my dad replied, "God. Don't tell them you are Palestinian. Tell them you are Syrian. Or, Lebanese." These were words I had never really heard before.

So I went back to school and when confronted again, I

replied, "Well, I am cereal but I think my mom is a Lesbian."

That joke put in the context of a group of jokes related to growing up as an Arab American child in American culture started to grow into a five-minute routine.

Next, I expanded my search through my experiences.

The obvious one is that I am Palestinian and my wife, Alison, is Jewish. So I developed another routine that explored the humorous side of a Palestinian who is married to someone who is Jewish.

These contrasts create the most surprises for audiences that conflict with what they expect and make the punch-lines that much more funny.

"Alison and I met in a town called Cicero which has a large Hispanic and Italian community," I'd explain. "Alison thought I was Mexican and I thought she was a very cheap Italian. ... We had 900 people at our wedding. We only sent out 24 invitations. We had all the Arab relatives on one side of the wedding ceremony and all the Jewish relatives on the other. We didn't have a bridal party, we had a UN peacekeeping force right down the center aisle. And the relatives were flicking pita bread and Matzoh bread at each other the whole time, arguing over who invented Hummus."

Adding the appropriate pause to a routine also emphasizes the humor. And I pause, and then look at the audience, and conclude, "And, there were 38 casualties at our wedding. They took one Jew and 37 Arabs at the reception to the hospital."

Today, I have a 90-minute standup comedy act and enough jokes to fill up 75 pages of material.

If someone handed me the 75 pages of material and said memorize this and I'll put you on stage, it never would have worked.

But there is an inherent "memory" that comes from developing material from your own life, and then "bulking it up" with new material that naturally spins off the other jokes.

In other words, you don't have to spend much time memorizing material that comes so naturally to you because you lived it.

But, you do have to appreciate cadence, delivery. Pause. Contrast.

And this is most important: If you have to explain basic facts of a joke to an audience, they won't get it. And when they do, it won't be funny.

Practice makes perfect.

189

Comedy Road Remains Bright

Since entering standup comedy as a partner career to journalism and column writing, I've learned to make my column writing funnier, too.

It has its moments. I wonder if audiences have a difficult time when I shift gears from serious columnist to comedy writer? When they laugh with me on stage, do they take my more serious writing seriously?

I don't know the answer. But I do know that standup comedy, like journalism, still requires good writing and good story telling talents. It has its differences, too. It is less about accuracy and more about clean, clear delivery.

Sorting through all that is not as challenging as one might think. You are either an honest journalist, or you are not. My serious columns remain true to the perspective I believe is accurate and most compelling. You don't adjust facts in columns to pander to personal opinion.

You can be more loose with the facts in comedy, however, as long as the point or punch-line is funny.

And I still get stupid questions and confront ignorant stereotypes, like the time a little old lady approached me with my book, "I'm Glad I Look Like a Terrorist: Growing Up Arab in America."

I leaned over to hear her soft voice when she said with the venom of a rattlesnake: "I can't believe you abandoned your Christian faith to become an Arab."

Now not even humor can help set that lady's anger straight.

And by the way, if you do run into my wife, don't tell her I am a Palestinian. She thinks I'm Puerto Rican.

I believe the future is only the past again, entered through another gate.

Arthur Wing Pinero

Onward

Like I've said, columnists are strange and inexplicable people, and many would apply the same adjectives to the founding of their careers. Happily, I've veered onto their highway, which led to my writing humor, religion, and lifestyle columns. Sharing my observations with readers and getting paid for it sometimes leaves me slack-jawed with pleasant surprise.

And just when I thought I didn't deserve any more gifts to open, in 2006 Art Buchwald defied death with a miraculous recovery from kidney failure and left hospice to write about his experience in his book, *Too Soon to Say Goodbye,* before his actual death in early 2007.

But back in 2006 when things first looked grim for him, I stayed with Art and his family for two days at hospice and wrote a column about it. I never meant it for publication. It was a report to my board written in column form, but Bob Haught encouraged me to take it further. It first ran in *Editor & Publisher,* and later on major journalism sites and newspapers and aired on Boston NPR.

The overwhelming response to my column surprised me, which leads me to hope, "I guess there's more to come."

This column embodies all the lessons I learned from fellow columnists.

The Final Days of Art Buchwald: A Visit

By Suzette Martinez Standring
Editor & Publisher, March 4, 2006

Milton, Mass. Renowned columnist Art Buchwald has refused dialysis, and it's only a matter of time, maybe a short time, before he dies. For a man awaiting The Reaper, he's in unusually fine fettle.

I spent two days by his side to find Buchwald doesn't see himself as courageous, nor does he feel shored up by supernatural spiritual strength. To fade away naturally is the decision he made when faced with the alternative of being hooked up to a dialysis machine three times a week, for five hours at a stretch for the rest of his life.

He said, "I had two decisions. Continue dialysis, and that's boring to do three times a week, and I don't know where that's going, or I can just enjoy life and see where it takes me."

I had come to his Washington D.C. hospice to present to him the 2006 Ernie Pyle Lifetime Achievement Award from the National Society of Newspaper Columnists. He was due to be honored at our Boston conference in June, but now his appearance isn't likely.

I offered to bring it to Washington to lift his spirits and to let him know in person how highly his NSNC colleagues regarded him.

Cathy Crary, his assistant, suggested I "come sooner than later." She picked me up at Dulles Airport and during our drive to hospice, she talked about her friendship and career with him since 1984, his great heart, and his accessibility through the years.

"He's listed in the phone directory and always has been. People see his name and can't believe it's the real Art Buchwald, but that's how he is," she said.

His daughter, Jennifer Buchwald, lives in Massachusetts not far from me. She and I are new friends and now she stays close by her father in hospice. Her dad had been "holding court" with a steady stream of visitors over the past two weeks. Jennifer invited me to stay an extra day with her, since it offered more chance for an audience with the king of political satire, now the newly crowned king of The Washington Home hospice.

February 28, the day I arrived, would have marked

the fourth week since he stopped dialysis. That can't be good. Would I arrive in time? What condition would he be in?

"Raucous" came to mind when Crary and I stepped through the glass doors around 9:30 a.m. and found him in the middle of a lively gab with Eunice and Maria Shriver, laughing it up over old memories and private jokes that bubbled up like champagne. Jennifer was there, as was Buchwald's son Joel, his wife Tamara and their two small children.

I felt a bit the interloper when things quieted down for brief introductions, but Buchwald brought the energy back up with, "Let me tell you just one more story..." It's obvious a "good dish" with his friends has him twinkling with happiness.

Art, in a blue and white striped golf shirt and blue sweat pants, wore a black tennis shoe on his left foot. His other pant leg hung loosely where his right leg has been amputated below his knee, but he gave no hint of pain or discomfort.

At a certain point, Jennifer announced, "Suzette's going to give him an award." It was akin to cake time at a birthday party. Everyone clapped their hands and said, "Ooh! An award!"

I didn't know what was more nerve wracking, trying to remember my little speech or having Eunice and Maria Shriver staring at me not two feet away. Pulling the plaque out, I stood up and said, "Art, I bring you national greetings from your friends, fans and colleagues at the National Society of Newspaper Columnists. We want to present you with our 2006 Ernie Pyle Lifetime Achievement Award.

"As you can see, Ernie Pyle's likeness graces the plaque because we consider him to be our patron saint, a legendary columnist who brought a human face to World War II with his stories about our soldiers, simply and profoundly told.

"And in the tradition of extraordinary columnists, you've shined a light on the politics of humanity. In that sense, you've been patron saint of political satire for almost six decades and we revere you.

"I bring congratulations and best wishes from the National Society of Newspaper Columnists." Everybody clapped and Art nodded his thanks.

Maria Shriver said, "Patron saint of political satire. I

like that. See Art? You can be a saint."

After they left, I found myself hanging out in hospice with Art and his family. He looks great and still enjoys his food, which is a good sign. It was pure pleasure not having anything to do, but to eat whatever he wanted to eat, according to Buchwald. "His favorite breakfast is fruit parfait, mini-cinnamon buns and chocolate milk from McDonald's," said Tamara, his daughter-in-law.

NPR show host Diane Rehm had conducted a poignant interview with Buchwald regarding his decision to forego further medical intervention, which aired four days earlier on February 24. Buchwald's candor was stunning. It's said that when facing death, a man's life passes before him, and this man passed along his feelings to Rehm, including his fears (none), regrets (none) and any spiritual expectations (he's not sure, but probably none). Buchwald's number is coming up, and he wants to meet his fate squarely, sans any extraordinary means of delay, thank you very much.

He read through a fat folder of fan mail, which later, Jennifer shared with me. The emails, cards and letters saluted and supported him. Many were tapped out with tears, according to their senders. Strangers wrote with relief, as if Buchwald's decision to captain his own destiny gave them permission someday to do so, too.

The willingness to jump overboard and wave off any lifeboat seems quite courageous, but Buchwald was unimpressed with the idea of bravery.

"I hated dialysis because it had to do with sitting there for five hours. It had to do with time. Once I made up my mind, that was it," he told me.

"The end" is not taboo talk. In fact, Buchwald finds funny fodder in knock-knock-knocking on heaven's door.

A nurse comes up, "Mr. Buchwald, Tom Brokaw is on the line."

Buchwald takes the call, laughing, "Hey, I'm still here and I don't know why..."

No doubt about it. Buchwald is a celebrity patient at hospice. Not everyone gets letters from Neal Simon or daily visits from members of the Kennedy clan.

But hospice hasn't been the non-stop party it was two weeks ago, according to his daughter, at least not today, which was fairly quiet. Time can stretch out in the warm living room where he sits most of the time, napping.

Joel and his family visit three times a day. Jennifer quit school in Massachusetts to be with her father. Whenever he slept nearby, she and I read or wrote on our laptops. We took the occasional walk whenever her dad wanted something special, like a fruit parfait from McDonalds.

"You better go now, and you might be lucky to get the last one," Buchwald said.

The cold dessert perked him up and with no celebrities to compete with, I pulled up a chair and asked him questions, like, "Art, why aren't you afraid of death?"

"Because I don't know what it is and I don't have control over it," he said.

"If you met God, what would he say to you?"

"There may or may not be a God, but I'm not going to be the one who is going to give the answers. Every religion is telling us there's one God, but I'm not sure, so I'm not giving it a lot of thought," he said.

His daughter asked, "Dad, did you ever have a near death experience?"

Buchwald said, "Maybe during the war. It felt like near death in a foxhole when it was being mobbed. It wasn't a very pleasant thing."

"Here, at hospice, what thoughts bring you joy?" I asked.

"My children, the fact that it all came out pretty damn good. Making people laugh, getting joy out of that," he said.

Buchwald easily wrote about 8,000 columns during his career, according to Crary. He wrote three columns a week until about 1995, and penned two weekly until this past January. I asked, "Art, do you miss writing? I know you're not doing your columns anymore, but are there moments when you're here and you wish you could just tap out one more column?"

"No, not really. I wrote a column, a sad one to run the day after I go to heaven," he said.

I asked, "What would you tell any humor columnists who want to be the next Art Buchwald?"

He said, "You are what you are. At the time all these things happened to me, newspapers were a great thing. If I tried to do it now, I might not even succeed today. Newspapers don't look at columns the way they used to."

Through the wooden slats just outside the windows, afternoon slices of sun gave the room a warm, lazy feel. This hospice was his last stop. Was it an uncomfortable thought?

Buchwald remained upbeat, "You gotta be somewhere and this is a pretty good place." Then he added, "Now I'm going to sleep."

He snoozed amid gifts and mementos. A box arrived, a gourmet frozen dessert from a friend. Buchwald resembled a sleeping Buddha before a table of orchids, spring bouquets and baskets of potted flowers. Nearby, a white teddy bear wore a purple chapeau with a polka dotted ribbon and white feather, a gift from one of the Kennedy clan.

I pressed a button, and the little bear's head moved side to side and a baby voice sang, "You fill up my thenses like a night in a foresth."

"Hey, it's singing *Annie's Song* by John Denver and the bear has a lisp," I said to his daughter and we giggled.

Jennifer said, "When he dies, it's going with him." Her father will be cremated along with gifts and pictures of his family and closest friends.

Later Buchwald took a call from his business agent. Afterwards, I asked him, "Did you have a nice conversation?"

He said, "Yeah, I told him I'm amazed. There's no change."

I said, "Why are you amazed?"

"Because they said I'd be dead without dialysis. I'm not supposed to be doing this good," Buchwald said.

I said, "Maybe it's the power of positive thinking. Maybe you're being carried along on love."

Later, it was time to fly back to Boston. My departure coincided with the afternoon arrival of two Kennedy family members.

We all said hello, but now it was time for a goodbye kiss on the top of Art Buchwald's head.

He took my hand, "Thanks, honey, thanks for bringing the award."

"Art, any pearls of wisdom for all the columnists who love you?"

"Keep writing. Tell them to just keep writing," he said.

Index

American Press Institute 31
American Society of Journalists
   and Authors 64
Anders, Smiley 58, 133, 148
Anderson, Laird 119
Astor, Dave....................58, 169
Authors Guild 64

Barry, Dave 35, 93, 157, 167
Beckham, Beverly 71, 74
Bennett, Samantha 31. 96
Bete, Tim 57, 92
blog 69, 173
Bragg, Rick............................44
Branton, John........................32
Brasch, Walter 14, 146
Braude, Jim 179
Buchwald, Art 7, 23, 26,
   49, 57, 91, 97
Buska, Sheila 58
Bykofsky, Stu 57, 155, 158

Cameron, W. Bruce........88, 89,
   96, 165, 166, 169
Carter, Tim 163
Casey, Maura 115, 147, 156
Chartrand, David 22, 28, 33
Clark, Roy Peter....................22
comedy................................185
conflict 34
copyright..............................61
Copyright Clearance
   Center 59, 61

death threats 143
DeSilva, Bruce 45
DiSandro, Deb 162
Dowd, Maureen 30
Eagen, Margery 179
editors, working with........68, 96
endings..................................43
Epstein, Rick 22
Erma Bombeck Writers
   Conference 35, 37, 39,
   57, 99, 101, 103

ethics 144
focus......................................34

foreshadow............................40
Fuson, Ken............................45

Givhan, Robin 14, 133, 156
Goodman, Ellen 21, 56, 59

Hamill, Pete ..11, 23, 29, 65, 73
Hanania, Ray 185
Hart, Jack 45
Haught, Robert......................51
Herbert, Bob..........................31
Hicks, Marybeth 133
Holz, Duane and Todd 133
Huffington, Arianna........66, 173
Hull, Anne..............................43
humor 88

interviews 118
Ivins, Molly 13

Jackson, Derrick....................28
Jacoby, Jeff 41
Jarvis, Melissa 57
Jenkins, Simon....................176

Kaiser, Frank 58, 134
Kelly, Marguerite....................59
Kenneally, Christopher 59, 61
Koehler, Robert 168
Kristoff, Nick 77
Krupa, Gene..........................23

Langley, Jay 10
Lawson, Patti 133
lead 28
length of column....................48
Leonard, Mike 72
Lieber, Dave 31, 37, 49,
   56, 110, 147, 157
lifestyle columns....................99
Lopez, Steve 30, 78

Index

Marotta, Terry 99, 104
McCarty, Mary 19, 39, 103
McManus, Lisa 68, 12
McNay, Don 30
McPhee, John 43
Messenger, Tony 110
metro columns 101, 110
Miller, Jim 163
Morin, Mike..........................179
Murphy, Michael....................99

Narrative Journalism
  Conference 45
National Society of Newspaper
  Columnists 7, 10, 13, 29,
  73, 75, 89, 138, 173, 193
National Writers Union 64
Newcombe, Rick 166
niche columns 133
Nieman Foundation 45
Norman, Tony.......................56

O'Shaughnessy, Tracey 21,
  59, 123, 124, 148
opinion columns 115

Pitts, Leonard...........76, 80, 81
point of view 13
Pollock, Ben 145, 170
Portillo, Ernesto 57
Poynter Institute 43, 45, 75, 145
Pulfer, Laura............37, 99, 103
Pulitzer Prize 75

quote 43

radio 179
Reisman, Phil........................59
religion columns 121
Reynolds, Lindor 147
Rinehart, Karen 21
Robertsn, J. Michael 138
Rummo, Greg.......................74

Scanlan, Christopher "Chip"..43

Schwab, Gary.......................46
self-editing 71
speeches 140
St. Yves, Dan 170
Stanton, Sam 44
Stasowski, Jim 31, 72
Stocker, Carol....................133
syndication 165

Tammeus, Bill 34, 49, 123,
  125, 147
Tan, L. Kim 19, 50, 65, 66
Tomlinson, Tommy 46
Tucker, Cynthia 30

Van Ostrand, Maggie 74
Vingle Fuller, Karin 99
voice...................................18

Waters, George 24
Will, George 167
Wilson, Craig.................33, 48,
  57, 72, 101
Woods, Keith 75
writer's block 55

Yeoh, Oon ..14, 19, 51, 53, 134
Yount, David...............123, 131

Zezima, Jerry 89, 95
  68, 121

Suzette Martinez Standring is a syndicated columnist with GateHouse News Service. Her columns for *The Patriot Ledger's* (MA) Spiritual Life section appear twice a month. Her humor and lifestyle columns have run in other publications, such as *The Boston Globe* and *The Milton Times* (MA).

Suzette is a past president of the National Society of Newspaper Columnists, has appeared on Boston's National Public Radio station, and presents writing workshops nationally. A San Francisco native, she now lives near Boston with her husband David. Her crowning achievement is her daughter, Star.

On a slow day, she'll write about her little black dog, Mojo.